Praise for *33 Million People in the Room*

"Juliette Powell has provided a timely crash course on how to leverage your business's online presence. A must-read for any aspiring entrepreneur, activist, brand manager, or c-level executive."
—Jeffrey Stewart, Serial Technology Entrepreneur; Founder, Mimeo, Urgent Career, and Monitor110

"Reading Juliette Powell's book is like perusing the secret trade documents of the most connected social butterfly. Upon first meeting Juliette, she immediately grabbed me by the arm and introduced me to the most important person in the room. When you pick up her book, it's the same experience. She reaches through the pages and gives the reader entry to the halls of power through online networking."
—Amy Shuster, Editorial Producer, MSNBC

"Juliette knows her way around a social network; she regales us with tales and practical advice from the plastic porous mediascape of today."
—David Thorpe, Global Director of Innovation, Ogilvy & Mather

"If you are in business or starting one, and wonder what the heck all this talk about social networking is about, this book is the best quick guide I've seen. It's full of juicy stories, backed up by sound social science, lucidly explained."
—Howard Rheingold, Author, *Smartmobs*; Professor, Stanford and Berkeley

"The exciting new world of online social networking is demonstrating the profound power of these truths to change the very fabric of society as we know it. Our interactions, relationships, and values are changing faster than most of us can comprehend. For some, the pace of this change is alarming. For others it is empowering. In *33 Million People in the Room* Juliette Powell takes us on a fun-filled tour of this rapidly changing hypo-manic digital ecosystem simultaneously providing both practical advice and an insightful commentary on the increasing importance of authenticity in modern culture. Along the way we meet a hilarious cast of characters and gain a behind-the-scenes glimpse into real social networking success stories showing how to leverage the power of this modern phenomenon to achieve meaningful social and economic results for you and your business."
—Michael Spencer, CTO, ASMALLWORLD

uliette Powell has brilliantly answered in rich dimensions *why* you should be deeply
ivolved in this new communications fabric. Through vignettes with the true leaders of
iis revolution, Juliette has set forth all the energy and steam you need for your boilers to
et going and enter the room."
-Chris Brogan, Business Advisor, chrisbrogan.com

uliette Powell has delivered a wonderfully succinct snapshot for embracing social
omputing as a way of doing business, not just the latest technology trend. Whether you
re new to making connections online or are a social computing technology veteran,
iliette encapsulates the themes, concepts, and ideas that are most relevant for anyone
i business interested in working in or exploring social computing."
-Jeffrey Dachis, Cofounder, Razorfish, Inc.; Cofounder, Senior Partner Bond Art &
:ience; Chairman, Producers Guild of America New Media Council

iocial networking is just not for breakfast anymore. *33 Million People in the Room*
emonstrates how it transcends marketing and promotion, connecting people and
ompanies in ways none of us dared dream. Thanks to Juliettte for putting this in
erspective, and to social networks for so many of my restless nights."
-David Blumenstein, Cofounder, The Hatchery

uliette Powell puts a human face on the social changes being wrought online,
hether describing new tools like MySpace and Facebook, or key concepts like viral
ommunication and social capital."
-Clay Shirky, Adjunct Professor, NYU's Graduate Interactive Telecommunications
rogram (ITP); Author, *Here Comes Everybody*

Ne all recognize that social networking and the technologies of connection and
ollaboration are an enormous phenomenon. But what do they mean? How can
iey, how will they be used to create social and economic value? Drawing on her
wn experience and on the insights of The Gathering Think Tank, Juliette Powell
as developed a powerful set of answers to those critical questions. Full of clear
xplanations, helpful examples, and accessible advice, *33 Million People in the Room* is
i important tool for managers and citizens alike—a sourcebook for the next economy."
-Lawrence Wilkinson, Cofounder and Vice Chair, Oxygen Media; Cofounder and
resident, Global Business Network; Cofounder and Chair, Heminge & Condell

uliette has done a terrific job of capturing the power of and the opportunities
resented by social networks. Whether you are looking to maximize the impact of 'You
ic' or a global company, there are important lessons in this book. Things have changed,
jain, and this book will help you capitalize on it."
-Doug Zingale, General Manager of Strategic Partnerships, Zune, Microsoft Corporation

"A nice introduction to an emerging global force that's still unfamiliar territory to many business people. It's a place where ideas can spread like wildfire and where great fortunes and even romances will be made and broken—yet no one is in charge. Depending on your perspective, what is described within this quick yet informative read is somewhere between a utopian future where everyone is connected as one—and the end of civilization as we know it."
—Bran Ferren, Chief Creative Officer, Applied Minds, Former President, Disney Imagineering, Creative Technology, and Disney R&D

"The network value of reading this book will be to increase your net value multifold, while thoroughly entertaining you with inside stories about the first social networking application, the uber-hip TED conference, and how an outspoken wine expert from New Jersey became an online micro-celebrity. *33 Million People in the Room* is a thoughtful, analytical and practical how-to for anyone looking to learn about social networking, from a budding blogger to a Fortune 500 CEO. I recommend reading this book or watching your back as others do."
—Dina Kaplan, Cofounder and COO, blip.tv

"I came into what was not yet called Cyberspace in 1985 searching for a new context for community...a new 'place' that might provide for the kind of essential human interdependencies that were the substrate of little agricultural towns like mine in Wyoming, now withering along with the family farm. Since then, despite the explosive settlement of the Electronic Frontier, this dream has felt to me increasingly like something forever in the future. But perhaps not. Juliette Powell provides evidence that the spark of collective life is starting to sustain itself in this vast and mysterious 'room' where all of us may gather. Her book is a dose of practical hope at a time when we need it."
—John Perry Barlow, Grateful Dead lyricist and cyberactivist

"Juliette Powell isn't just an expert in community, she lives it. Her ideas are a must for any person or company building a social network."
—Ori Brafman, *The New York Times* and *The Wall Street Journal* bestselling Author, *Sway* and *The Starfish and The Spider*

33 MILLION
PEOPLE
IN THE ROOM

33 MILLION PEOPLE IN THE ROOM

HOW TO CREATE, INFLUENCE, AND RUN A SUCCESSFUL
BUSINESS WITH SOCIAL NETWORKING

JULIETTE POWELL

Vice President, Publisher
Tim Moore

Associate Publisher and Director of Marketing
Amy Neidlinger

Editorial Assistants
Pamela Boland
Myseha Graham

Development Editor
Russ Hall

Operations Manager
Gina Kanouse

Digital Marketing Manager
Julie Phifer

Publicity Manager
Laura Czaja

Assistant Marketing Manager
Megan Colvin

Cover Designer
Stauber Design Studio

Managing Editor
Kristy Hart

Project Editor
Chelsey Marti

Copy Editor
Geneil Breeze

Proofreader
Water Crest Publishing

Indexer
Erika Millen

Compositor
Eric S. Miller

Manufacturing Buyer
Dan Uhrig

This book is dedicated to Napier Collyns, for challenging me to publish my ideas; and to my extended family—Guy Laliberté, Ron Dennis, Moses Znaimer, Bran Ferren, Art Chang; and to my mother, Marcelle Lapierre, and cousins Nicole, Michael Jr., and Ginger-Lei, all of whom continue to teach me the value in choosing people of quality in my life.

CONTENTS

FOREWORD BY NAPIER COLLYNS

Things are happening so fast. When I was a boy, only a handful of privileged people had phones and cars. The hand-delivered telegram was the quickest way to reach someone. Handwritten letters were treasured and often kept in perpetuity. Business was transacted in the same way. Fifty years ago, we used telexes to communicate between London and New York; the trans-Atlantic phone was too expensive. A few years later, we began to use faxes. And then in the early eighties, as electronic communication via personal computers emerged in academia, we adapted it in Shell for business purposes. At the same time, Stewart Brand started the Whole Earth 'lectronic Link (WELL) to enable an emerging intellectual and cultural elite in the San Francisco Bay Area to communicate with each other, exchanging ideas, news, jokes, and personal aspirations. Stewart went on to help us found Global Business Network (GBN) in 1987 to enable business leaders to share their knowledge and ideas with the "remarkable people" we had chosen to form a visionary team of advisers across many disciplines. Before the Internet as we now know it got started, we were already communicating continuously through our private corner of the WELL. Increasingly businesses and governments began to use the new channels of communication for collaborative thinking, decision-making, and speed of action.

One day about four years ago, I received an e-mail from Juliette Powell asking to meet me. She had recently formed

The Gathering Think Tank with a group of young entrepreneurial leaders in technology, media, policy, art, science, innovation, and business. I told her about our aspirations in forming GBN—to bring together leaders of major corporations with prominent and exceptional thinkers, artists, and innovators who could share their knowledge and instincts about where the world was going and ways to respond. The idea was to create scenarios of the future that would help business leaders imagine different possibilities and share an intuitive sense of where things might be headed. Juliette and I were "e-introduced" through a mutual acquaintance who insisted that The Gathering Think Tank was the twenty-first century version of GBN and its "remarkable people." He went on to say that of all the founders of GBN she should meet me, because she was ostensibly "the next generation Napier Collyns"!

With Juliette's knowledge in media, new media, and technology and my experience of getting leaders to sit down and engage with the ideas of other people, we began to explore new ways of collaborating and doing business. So many new methods of exchanging information, ideas, and beliefs—both publicly and privately—had been developed through the proliferation of electronic communications that it was now possible to instantly share ideas with literally millions of people or just the few or the one you select. Juliette seemed to have all this in her head both from personal experience and from a kind of instinctual grasp!

That's why I wanted Juliette to write this book: To help people, old and young, to participate in this new business and learning opportunity. She started teaching my colleagues and me to take advantage of the new social networking tools, which have helped us in our business as well in our personal lives. Now her book delivers those critical lessons to a much broader audience. Every single reader will learn something new, and each of us—from corporate executives to college graduates just starting their careers—will apply that knowledge in different ways. I am sure Juliette would be happy to coach any company that wants to dive deeper into this new world with greater confidence and craft and implement a tailor-made, winning social media strategy. As you read this book, you will see how these amazing new ways of social networking can lead you to more innovative and effective ways of doing business and staying connected.

Napier Collyns spent thirty years as an international energy executive. In 1987, he cofounded Global Business Network, now a member of Monitor Group, with Peter Schwartz, Stewart Brand, Jay Ogilvy, and Lawrence Wilkinson.

FOREWORD BY JIMMY WALES AND ANDREA WECKERLE

Wikipedia—a strange word no one had ever heard before it was coined in 2001. Today, less than eight years later, it is estimated that nearly one billion people have used the website. For many of them, Wikipedia has become a household word. Building a global brand like that, instantly recognizable by hundreds of millions of people, traditionally took decades and tens or hundreds of millions of dollars in marketing.

However, in creating and building Wikipedia into a household brand, the Wikimedia Foundation, the charity Jimmy founded to operate the project, spent nothing on marketing. Not one cent. Wikipedia essentially grew by word of mouth, as the excitement felt within the Wikipedia community spread one person at a time to bloggers and web masters, who in turn spread it to their readers, and their friends, and their mothers, and so on and on and on.

Using examples like this one and others featured in *33 Million People in the Room,* Juliette Powell explains how businesses, large and small, are using modern online tools to cut through the clutter and reach their audience in new ways. Powell outlines how the use of social networks will help readers expand their business, reduce risks, and reduce costs—whether they are entrepreneurs at a small business just starting out, the marketing manager for a stable business that is decades old, or the CEO of a Fortune 500 company doing something as high

XVI	33 MILLION PEOPLE IN THE ROOM

tech as creating semiconductors, or as low tech as operating a corner wine shop.

In addition to discussing some of today's most useful social networking tools and explaining how they are relevant to different situations, she drives home the point that every individual has the ability to increase their *social capital*—the network of relationships and the resources available and accessible therein—and their *cultural capital*—the influence and corresponding advantages resulting from that person's knowledge, experience, and connections—which in turn have a positive effect on an individual's ability to increase his or her financial capital.

Amidst the tech and consumer examples she uses to illustrate her points, Powell also throws in bits of fascinating information such as the UCLA and Boradex study that discusses the correlation between a company's highly networked employees and the ability of that company to make better policy decisions and investments and therefore improve its bottom line.

Notably, some of the book's most historically interesting sections involve recent United States politics. One recent example is Barack Obama's 2008 win of the U.S. Presidency, where Powell dissects Obama's internet campaign:

> *"The runaway success of Obama's internet campaign rests primarily on three key factors, first among them a significantly larger financial investment in the online arena than those of his opponents. Obama's campaign*

spent 10 to 20 times more on banner ads and sponsored links than his fellow candidates, running ads across a wide array of sites ranging from large newspapers like the Boston Globe to political blogs like Daily Kos and the Drudge Report. The second key factor in the campaign's success was its lack of direct, in-your-face sales approaches. Clicking on an Obama banner ad led users not to a donation page, but rather to a form where they could sign up for campaign event invitations. Only after submitting the form were visitors asked to make a donation. By avoiding outright sales tactics, Obama confirmed his sincerity and sent supporters a clear, though unspoken, message: allegiance is more important than money. The third factor of Obama's campaign, and the one that would take his message from a core group of ardently devoted followers and straight into the general public, lay in his deep understanding of the online world."

The other is Al Gore's still controversial loss of the bid for Presidency in 2000:

"In the United States presidential election of 2000, Al Gore won the popular vote but ultimately, thanks to a decision handed down by the Supreme Court, lost to Republican candidate George W. Bush. The defeat was humiliating, but through it, Gore would learn an invaluable lesson; one that would ultimately help him to change the course of history. With the defeat of Gore the politician, Gore the man could stop thinking about how he was supposed to act and start just being

*himself.... Perhaps the real key to Gore's success in
creating such widespread awareness [of global warming]
was in a combination of his ability to passionately
and convincingly communicate what he knew on the
one hand, and on the other, in his shrewd ability to
disseminate his message through his vast personal social
network as well as to the multitudes of people who knew
about him."*

33 Million People in the Room is a slender book, but don't
underestimate its importance just because it is less than 200
pages. Lots of business-type books are dry as a bone, but
this one is engaging and fun to read. It can help you learn to
do what Jimmy did with Wikipedia—for yourself, or for your
business or charity. If you don't understand the social nature of
the web and make use of it to be successful, your competitors
most certainly will.

*Jimmy Wales, Founder of Wikipedia and Andrea Weckerle,
Communications Consultant & Entrepreneur
New York City, Autumn 2008*

ACKNOWLEDGMENTS

Like every other big decision in my life, I began writing this book after a mentor challenged me to do so. I could not have foreseen how much of a challenge it would actually be to complete. About seven months into the development of *33 Million People in the Room*, right around the time the first draft was due, I discovered a lump in my chest. After a series of painful tests and a stint at the Mayo Clinic, I was diagnosed with fibroid abnoma. As my mother always says: "It isn't what happens to you in life that matters, it's what you choose to do with it!" In this case, I chose to say YES! to life, and my diagnosis became a motor to the successful completion of this book.

33 Million People in the Room wouldn't have been possible without the invaluable contribution and friendship of hundreds of people, and in particular, that of Sophy Bot. What began as a close friend patiently listening to my ideas over the course of nine months evolved in the last month of writing into a flourishing collaboration and a lifelong friendship. Sophy's adept and cheerful ability to clarify my ideas, organize them, and tie them all together in a way that readers of all levels could easily understand made all the difference in readying this book for publication on time and in difficult circumstances. With her penchant for unruly robots, she also demonstrated an uncanny ability to make me laugh as she guided this book from nonsense to sense. Against all odds and impossible time lines, I couldn't have wished for a better co-conspirer.

ABOUT THE AUTHOR

Juliette Powell is a social media expert and Founder of The Gathering Think Tank, Inc. (http://www.thegatheringwebsite.com), an innovation forum that connects technology, media, entertainment, and business communities.

Her decade long career began as a teenager, working in live broadcast television and naturally expanded into interactive/new media content and formats, bolstered by a lifelong interest in people and community-building.

With her deep knowledge of the people and technologies at the forefront of social media, Powell, a serial entrepreneur, has gained a solid reputation for discovering the latest developments and distilling their social and business implications. Her consulting services have been employed by corporate, government, and new media organizations, including Red Bull, Mozilla, Microsoft, Compaq, Trump International, Nokia, the United Nations, the Department of Justice, Paltalk, and Rocketboom.

She has served as a guest speaker at MIT's Innovation Forum, NYU's Interactive Technology Program, and the Producer's Guild of America's New Media Council. She has also assisted in the production of the world-renowned Technology, Entertainment, and Design (TED) Conference. Powell began her career as a television host, producer, and founder of Powell International Entertainment, Inc. (PIE, Inc.), an integrated media production and development company that produced special reports with newsmakers such as Nelson Mandela, Prince Charles, Sir Richard Branson, Steven Spielberg, and Tom Cruise. She also worked on projects with The Biography Channel, Women's Entertainment Television, E! Entertainment Television, Cirque du Soleil, and Bravo. Most recently, Powell created Canada's first cross-platform interactive show designed for TV, Internet, radio, and mobile applications.

Juliette is a dual citizen who lives in Manhattan, NY and maintains a residence in Montreal, Canada.

For more information about the author, visit juliettepowell.com

TWELVE MINUTES AND FORTY-EIGHT SECONDS WOULD DETERMINE WHETHER THE ENTIRE FRANCHISE WOULD MAKE IT OR GO BUST. FOR CHRIS ANDERSON, IT FELT A LITTLE LIKE WALKING INTO THE LION'S DEN.

CHAPTER 1

THE POWER OF SOCIAL NETWORKS

In February 2002, a collective of the world's top movers
and shakers sat in the front row of the auditorium: Jeffrey
Katzenberg, Quincy Jones, Art Buchwald, and Frank Gehry. A
bevy of other noteworthy luminaries stirred in their seats with
a mix of curiosity and anticipation as they awaited the opening
address from Anderson, TED's new vanguard.

For 12 years, the Monterey Convention Center had been
home to TED, the world-renowned conference known as a
critical incubating cradle for developments ranging from the
Macintosh computer to *Wired* magazine to the Human Genome
Project. Media moguls, scientists, and entertainers sit, listen,
and learn alongside Fortune 500 executives, venture capitalists,
and Nobel prize-winning laureates, comparing notes during
conversation breaks and returning to the auditorium to indulge
in new sessions and new inspiring ideas. In many ways, TED
is to technology what the Bohemian Club is to politics or
what Studio 54 was to fashion and music in the 1970's. And, in
that, TED is not unlike elite social networks as they have been
throughout human history. Where else would Matt Groening,
creator of *The Simpsons*, converse over coffee with Max
Levchin, a founder of PayPal, and follow it up by chatting with
Craig Venter, mapper of the human genome?

By the time Anderson reached center stage, the tension in the
room was palpable. The soft-spoken British-born journalist
and publisher represented a changing of the guard, a fresh start
with new ownership and new ideas. For some, it felt like the
beginning of the end of the TED they had grown to love. For
others, it was the dawn of a new era of possibility. Anderson
had his work cut out for him. The expectations were high, and

he had resolved to surpass them. But first, he had to convince a room filled with some of the most connected people on the planet that he was deserving and worthy of their trust.

Chris Anderson, the entrepreneurial icon, stepped onto the stage to reveal Chris Anderson, the man who admitted to be desperately searching for the key to his own happiness. He told the rapt room about how just a couple years before, those who met him as a TED attendee would have encountered a man who started with nothing and had grown into an ego-driven billionaire whose personal self-worth was completely wrapped up in the value of his financial net worth. In the height of the dot-com bubble bust, Anderson's net worth dwindled by about $1 million per day—for 18 months straight. He wasn't as concerned with the loss of the money as with the all-important question of, "How did I let my personal happiness get so tied up in this business thing?" Over an insubstantial span of time, he watched everything that he built over 15 years crumble to nothing. The story he recounted resonated with the audience, 90 percent of whom at one time during their respective careers had ridden the same terrifying rollercoaster.

Anderson paused and looked his new community in the eye before going on to explain how the need to alleviate the stresses around his emotional and financial tempests had brought him to invest in the future of TED. His sense of purpose echoed their common desire to use the conference as a catalyst for change, easing them all through the difficult transition by giving the community a place to co-create the future together. He said that the theme of the following year's conference was to be Rebirth, in honor of a community coming together in times of challenge and change. Among other changes afoot, Anderson planned to expand TED to represent more than the three original fields providing its namesake—Technology, Entertainment, and Design—to also encompass education, politics, literature, spirituality, science, energy, social entrepreneurship, and environmental issues, among other subjects. He also planned to propel the exclusive TED community of about 1,500 people into uncharted territory by opening it up to the world using the power of social networking platforms. Anderson's 12 minute and 48 second talk won him a standing ovation and a big thumbs-up to proceed with his vision for his newfound community.

As he promised when he took over back in 2002, TED has gone on to spawn new horizons and open up its closed-door policy to the world by embracing social technology and all its possibilities. Despite its success, this was a bold move—at $6,000 per invitation-only ticket, TED's community was considered to be one of the most exclusive and tightly woven in the world. Why should they embrace the idea of offering free access to just anyone who wants it? Besides that, TEDsters were not inclined to spend time in online social networks or discussion groups—they simply didn't have the time or the perceived need.

The arrival of June Cohen as head of TED's media and online initiative changed all that and brought TED into a new era of open communication. Cohen understood that whether they were technicians, volunteers, celebrities, or sponsors, just about everyone who experiences a session at TED wants to talk about it. In 2006, she began a mass experiment aimed at distributing free sponsored online video of the archived TEDtalks. Over the next two years, the TEDtalk videos would be viewed more than 50 million times, generating a fierce TED community of self-selected individuals, the majority of which will never attend the conference itself. By opening TED up to social networking platforms, Cohen and Anderson had played to a natural human phenomenon—the innate desire to be part of a community. *33 Million People in the Room* is about understanding that need, codifying it, and using that code to better succeed in business.

FROM "CATCHING UP" TO "STAYING IN TOUCH" ·

THE NEW ORDER FAVORS THOSE WHO NETWORK, CREATE BUZZ, AND PROMOTE THEIR BRAND. EVEN IF THE BUBBLE BURSTS—AND WE PREDICT IT WILL—THE POWER OF SOCIAL MEDIA TO TRANSFORM OUR BUSINESSES AND SOCIETY WILL ONLY GROW.
—NEWSWEEK

From MySpace to Facebook and LinkedIn to Webkinz, social networks are all over news headlines and everyone is talking about them. The question is: What are they, and why do they matter? And, more importantly, how do they apply to you and your business?

The concept of a social network goes back long before the Internet (or for that matter, the personal computer) was ever invented. It refers to a community in which individuals are somehow connected—through friendship, values, working relationships, ideas. Nowadays the term **social network** also refers to a Web platform where people can connect with one another. It's the online counterpart of the rolodex and card catalog wrapped into one, and it's becoming just as ubiquitous. Online social networks are in essence just offering new ways to communicate. Where once we sent letters, then we made phone calls, then we e-mailed and sent text messages, now we connect through our online profiles and become friends with each other on Facebook.

Think about all the jobs you've had, all the schools you've attended, and all the friends and colleagues you've made along the way, and imagine still being able to get in touch with all of them. Maybe that former colleague's recommendation would help you land that job. Or maybe your college buddy's startup is willing to support your company's latest initiative. Social networks aren't just about catching up—they're about staying in touch.

When you look at the history of business, art, and science, the people who are changing the cultural, business, and scientific landscape are all connected to each other. In any era, the great artists and the brilliant scientists all knew each other. They got together and inspired each other and collaborated together. Social networks make those relationships transparent and provide tools to help you connect and *stay* connected.

Whether you're from a small organization or a large corporation, social networks are changing the world and the way we do business. Anybody can join them for free, and they're creating new business opportunities in production, distribution, and communication. They offer low barriers to entry and a bevy of potential revenue-generating possibilities. How are you going to seize these opportunities and make money, whether you are a small mom-and-pop shop or a large multinational?

REED'S LAW AND THE CENTER OF THE UNIVERSE

It's become a seamless part of the standard business lunch—sitting down at the table, pulling in your chair, taking out your smartphone, and placing it on the table in front of you. Everybody in the restaurant does the same. The conversations may be face-to-face, but the presence is worldwide. With each smartphone comes a world of contacts—phone numbers, e-mail addresses, social networking profiles. Each device connects the dots between the people at the table and their extended network of friends and associates, both online and off. There may only be two people at the table, but there are *33 Million People in the Room.*

When Chris Anderson and June Cohen opened up TED's online social network and expanded their community into the millions, they were building on a concept called Reed's Law. The law, created by Internet "uncle" David Reed, states that the effectiveness of large networks (and social networks in particular) can scale exponentially with the size and social

importance of the network. In other words, Reed suggests
that every new person on a network doubles its value. Let's go
back to the restaurant and say that between you, your lunch
partner, and all the contacts in both of your phones, you have a
network of 25 individuals. According to Reed's Law, the amount
of possible connections and subgroups within your group
of 25 individuals is an astonishing *33 million*. Add just five
more individuals to your network and the amount of possible
connections shoots all the way up to a billion. Reed's law
explains why social networks have literally exploded onto the
scene, but more importantly, it shows the vast potential offered
therein. When each new addition to a network doubles its value,
the revenue-generating possibilities multiply pretty quickly.

Take for example the first social networking application
for collaborative research and development to incorporate
pregenerated expert profiles. With more than 1.4 million
biomedical experts from more than 150 countries, the
BioMedExperts site currently houses approximately 12 million
preestablished network connections, none of which were
uploaded by a human. Each of these connections between
people, ideas, and areas of interest was automatically generated
from more than six million scientific publications from 6,500
journals, and experts can access the system to revise and/or
update their personal details, publications, and/or preferences.
As a biomedical research scientist who blogs under the name
DrugMonkey wrote in a June 23, 2008, post: "Obviously
the serious geekery part is starting with your own cloud of
connections and seeing what it can tell you… the database
allows a little more broad-based research which is where it
comes in handy as a networking tool, among other things."

The open platform also reflects the real-life activity network of experts worldwide even as the social tools enable them to connect in the virtual world.

Of course, not every scientist invited to join the BioMedExperts online network will participate, let alone create a subgroup within the larger network, just as not every possible subgroup calculated by Reed's law will emerge and be fruitful. For every person who does not join the network, the value of the network will be exponentially diminished. Fair enough, since it is in the potential value of the connections that *do* form that you want to invest your time, energy, and resources. But are all connections created equal, or are some connections more important than others?

A joint study by researchers at UCLA and Boardex, a corporate social networking platform, looked at how being right in the center of a network affects the financial success of that company. The conclusion is obvious, but not for the reason you might expect. You'd think that the reason the company would do well is because everyone would recognize them as the center of their "universe," and they'd have bigger brand awareness, a larger market, more sales, and increased revenue. What you might not expect is that being positioned in the center actually gives you more information, and it's the information that then gives you power.

The center of the universe study shows what you might expect: Companies are influenced by their social connections. Surprisingly, it also provides scientific evidence to suggest that these companies are empowered to exploit their competitive position in the network. Being in the center means that your company makes better policy decisions and better investments, and those advantages improve your bottom line.

The idea that a company can be the center of the universe for its industry is pretty heady, especially when it means being the hub of information for those around you. The revelation that the more a company hires highly networked employees, the better chance the company has at being the center of its industry's network is even more impressive. Changes within the company occur not only when a director and key executive are hired or fired, but also when they develop new connections by sitting on a new board of directors, by joining new organizations, and by using social technology to leverage their relationships. Connected people are hubs of information, and they have an enormous impact on both the inner workings of a company and on how other firms perceive the company. Think of it as if you were planning a party. The most memorable parties aren't the ones that have the best location or the best music. The best parties, and the best companies for that matter, are the ones that have the most interesting mix of people.

But what happens when highly connected people leave a network? The center of the universe study answered that question by looking at the impact that the death of a highly connected corporate decision maker could have on the life and performance of the company it served. To do that, the UCLA researchers tracked more than 2,000 firms and 30,000 key executives from 2000 to 2006. Not surprisingly, the study determined that when highly connected people die, so too do the connections between their companies.

The study demonstrates that companies that influence the culture around the firm's larger business community are positioned more centrally in the network and are, in turn, highly influenced by the culture around them. Being at the heart of the business hub leads to better decisions because companies are exposed to a wider set of information than their less networked counterparts. The more pertinent information you have access to, the better the decisions you are likely to make and the better your company is likely to run.

Researchers also uncovered another compelling reason to be in the center of the universe, so to speak. The team focused on directors who actively positioned themselves right in the heart of their business networks, and as you might imagine, they found strong evidence to suggest that the more connected the director, the more she was compensated. After all, in business, it's not just about *what* you know. It's also about *who* you know and how well you use those relationships.

So far, we've seen that a company's social networking capabilities and the active networking of its employees have an impact on everything from the inner workings of boards to the influence they amass in the larger business community. But what if you are a well-connected slacker with a lot of cultural appeal—someone who doesn't produce real value for the company, but who is well liked by all? Would you still receive higher compensation than your less connected colleagues? To find that out, researchers Nguyen and Dang took the center of the universe hypothesis one step further by looking at the French elite. They discovered that not only are socially well-connected CEOs more likely to make more money, they are also far less likely to be fired for poor performance, and, amazingly, they were more likely than their unconnected peers to find new and solid employment when they were shown the door.

NEW OPPORTUNITIES IN COMMUNICATION, PRODUCTION, AND DISTRIBUTION

Online social networks are no substitute for face-to-face interactions. Their strength lies in allowing you to collect information about the network you *already* have. The technology lifts the veil off of preexisting relationships when connections hidden or lost over time are suddenly revealed. It also allows you to extend your network to individuals who are just outside your personal network but with whom you share common friends, colleagues, and ideas. Social networks provide the tools to control the information flow between you and your network, and can help you yield more from your relationships with other people. Imagine how amplifying your ability to connect with people and maintain relationships could create a competitive advantage and higher economic performance for you and your company.

As my friend John Perry Barlow reminded me, a few generations ago, there were a lot of people in the railroad business who didn't realize that what they really did was transportation. So when the airline business came around, they didn't have the sense to get into it. You have the same thing here. None of the current winners in business are going to win in the next 30 to

40 years if they don't have the sense to invest in and harness the power of social networks.

The new and open world of socially enabled business provides greater opportunities and more chances to succeed. For most companies, the opportunities tend to be centered in the realms of communication, production, and distribution. Improve your communication by opening the channels both within your company and externally, and you improve the relationship between you and your community. Enhance your distribution abilities by taking advantage of the often viral nature of message dissemination and the natural tendency of online communities to cluster into dedicated groups. Develop new possibilities for production using technology that allows your preexisting community to work with each other on products that can benefit your company directly. Learn the natural order of the socially networked world and then decide how to get out there and make it work for you and your business.

"WHAT DO YOU DO?" SAID THE OFFICERS AT THE US-CANADA BORDER AS THEY PROCESSED HER VISA APPLICATION. SUDDENLY, CANADIAN EXPATRIATE TARA HUNT FOUND HERSELF BEING GOOGLED. THE AMUSED REACTION OF THE BORDER PATROL OFFICERS TO THEIR SEARCH QUERY SPOKE

CHAPTER 2
GETTING ON AND GETTING STARTED

volumes: "You should state on your resume that you're very Google-able!"

Social networking isn't just used for Tara Hunt's business. It *is* her business. Her company, Citizen Agency, consults clients on how to better connect with their customer communities. Whether through existing social networks, building more tools on brand Web sites to engage people, or just by making them aware of the rapidly changing marketplace, Tara guides her clients through the online networking space. She became an expert in the field after she began using social networks as a personal lifestyle tool in Canada and intuited that their powerful feedback mechanisms could also be at the service of business. When Tara moved to San Francisco a few years ago, she barely' knew anybody. It was then that she began using social networks to make friends, create community, and start a new business.

"My social networking strategy is pretty simple," she advises. "Just get out there as much as you can and build bridges. Interact. Take photos with high-profile people both in your industry and beyond. Post the photos, tag them, blog, and join discussion groups. Comment on other people's highly read postings and sign off with an embedded link to your site."

While techno-savvy marketing people might find this obvious, Tara also knew that she could not rely on Internet tools alone. Digital literacy is one thing; it allows you to use online social tools that help you reach a wider audience and maintain preexisting relationships. However, to be truly successful in the social networking space, digital literacy and social skills

need to go hand in hand. If you really want to start getting to
know people in your local area and, more importantly, if you
want them to know you, getting out to conferences and meet-
ups is mandatory. Tara understood that while online tools are
all-important, there is still no substitute for meeting people in
person.

During her forays into the online and offline worlds, Tara found
that most companies she encountered had no idea how to
connect with and broaden their community and customer base.
She saw and seized a business opportunity. Her personal use of
social networks was slowly bringing in new clients, and by now
she was in a position where she could propose these same tools
as an added value to her customers.

The unexpected part about Tara's business strategy emerged
later in her experimentation with the different tools and
strategies used in social networks: "I probably do *more* free
work now than I did in the beginning." While the concept of
working for free may seem foreign at first, just ask any intern
why he's willing to do it. When beginning a career, you're more
than willing to work for free to prove your value before officially
going on board. Or take product sampling—if you try my
chocolate bar and you like it, the dollar I spent giving away that
one bar will pay back with dividends if you start buying a few a
week (not to mention if your friends have a sweet tooth too). It's
the same thing online. Tara realized that by doing some client
work free of cost, there would be an inevitable payback worth
far more than the initial investment of nonbillable hours. After
all, the best way to create a meaningful and fruitful connection

with potential customers and clients is to do free favors for them.

Nowadays, Tara lands paid speaking engagements all over the world and has developed a great network of friends and clients both nationally and internationally. In her own words, "I don't need a resume anymore. Just Google me. That's a pretty powerful position to be in when one is looking for a good job or new clients." And Tara's results really do speak for themselves, whether in the business world or at the US-Canada border—go ahead, Google her!

WHAT IS THIS KID'S STUFF?

DO BUSINESS AS IF YOU WERE PLAYING A GAME. HAVE FUN, KNOW THE RULES, AND WHEN IT'S TIME, MAKE UP YOUR OWN.
—GUY LALIBERTE, FOUNDER AND CEO, CIRQUE DU SOLEIL

So your daughter's buying a better igloo on Club Penguin and your son is showing off his band's latest song on MySpace while you, for your part, are posting your resume to business networking tool LinkedIn. Great, you're all online and using social networks. Should you now be worried that your daughter's penguin and your son's demo might somehow pop up when somebody's looking through your work history and colleague recommendations? The simple answer is no, not really. That's because different types of networks exist for different audiences and different purposes, and each is a microcosm unto itself. There is no "one size fits all" solution to social networking, and each network is created with different uses and users in mind. A fundamental understanding of the differences between the networks is key to making the best use of the tools that are already out there and to finding the best tool to suit your needs and the needs of your business. What follows is a rundown of the biggest social networks today along with the main ones that you should be watching.

MySpace

www.myspace.com

Number of users: 114 million

Growth rate: 230,000+ new users per day

Founded: 2003

Primary audience: Musicians, teenagers, culture-at-large

Best used for: Promotion of mass market products, music, and celebrities; Community building among younger audiences; Trend spotting and testing

It's been called the biggest disruptive force to hit pop culture since MTV and the biggest mall, nightclub, and 7-Eleven parking lot ever created. Self-touted as "A Place for Friends," Rupert Murdoch-owned MySpace is home to more than 114 million users and continues to expand at an astounding rate of 230,000 new users every day. The majority of the audience is comprised of independent musicians and their fans, many of whom were turned onto the network because of the robust music tools featured on the site. Teenagers have also logged on to the site en masse as have many general Internet users looking for a way to connect and keep up with friends. While the ability to upload and stream music tracks is a key feature, other primary features of MySpace include customizable profiles, blogs, bulletin boards, and classifieds. While MySpace may be known as the goliath of social networks, a new rival has quietly come from behind to surpass it in the number of monthly unique visitors.

Facebook

www.facebook.com

Number of users: 124 million

Growth rate: 250,000+ new users per day

Founded: 2004

Primary audience: General Internet users, international audience, users aged 25-34 and 35+

Best used for: Building and maintaining your personal network; Promotion of mass market products, music, and celebrities/politicians; Community building among older audiences; Trend spotting and testing

Facebook was launched in 2004 as a closed social network exclusively for students of Harvard University. The network turned out to be an immediate success, enrolling half the undergraduate community within the first month alone. Over the next two years, Facebook expanded to include other universities, high schools, and corporate networks, before finally opening up to the world at large (as long as that world was over 13 years old and had a valid e-mail address). Today Facebook boasts more than 124 million users and is growing at an unprecedented rate of 250,000 new users per day, much of that growth being centered outside the United States. Like its rival MySpace, Facebook generates revenue through banner advertising on the site and offers membership and features free of cost. A key feature on the site is the profile "wall," which allows users to post messages and comment on each another's activities. Facebook also features tools to update your personal status (that is, post a one- or two-sentence update on what you're up to); post photos, videos, notes, and links; post free events, classified ads, and product-based pages; and interact with friends via customized applications.

hi5

www.hi5.com

Number of users: 70 million

Growth rate: Up to 350,000 new users per day

Founded: 2003

Primary audience: Rated the #1 social network across 25 nations in Latin America, Europe, Asia, and Africa

Best used for: Promotion of mass market products, music, and celebrities and community building outside the United States

Rated one of the top 20 most visited sites on the Web, Hi5 is one of the world's largest social networks. Most of its users are based outside the United States, and the network supports more than 27 languages. It is particularly popular in Latin America, Portugal, Romania, and Cyprus. Profile features on the site include journals, photos, groups, and applications. With 56 million individual monthly visitors and spikes of up to 350,000 new users signing up in a single day, Hi5 is among the largest social networks internationally and continues to expand at one of the fastest rates on the Web today.

Orkut

www.orkut.com

Number of users: 120 million

Founded: 2004

Primary audience: General Internet users mainly located in Brazil and India

Best used for: Promotion of mass market products, music, and celebrities to audiences in Brazil and India

"Bad, bad server. No donut for you," reads an error message on Orkut, a self-described "online community designed to make your social life more active and stimulating." Orkut's lighthearted approach echoes the attitude of its creator, Orkut Büyükkökten, a Google engineer, who in 2004 launched the network in the United States but soon found it flooded with users from Brazil and India. Heeding their shifting audience, Google announced that Orkut would be fully managed and operated in Brazil as of August 2008. Orkut demonstrates a key point in building custom social networks: While a site may be built with a particular community in mind, creating a site does not automatically predict the audience that will inhabit it. Orkut features include profiles, communities, and applications, as well as a scrapbooking feature that allows users to send and receive messages and images.

Bebo

www.bebo.com

Number of users: 40 million

Founded: 2005

Primary audience: Teens and young adults in the UK, Canada, Ireland, New Zealand, Australia, and Poland

Best used for: Promotion of mass market products, music, and celebrities to audiences outside the United States; Community building among teens and young adults

AOL's 2008 acquisition of Bebo cemented its role as one of the big players in the world of social networks. It is currently the top social network among teens and young adults in the UK, Ireland, and New Zealand but also houses a fair amount of US-based users. Though currently home to younger users, expansion plans are aimed at targeting a wider demographic. Bebo operates using an open application platform, making it easier for developers to create and launch new applications on the site. Key functionality of Bebo includes robust music, author, and group features. The site has experienced slow and steady growth and has the potential for wide expansion if its tools can be fully exploited.

Twitter

www.twitter.com

Number of users: 2 million

Growth rate: 3,500 new users per day

Founded: 2006

Primary audience: Heavy and highly connected Internet users

Best used for: Expanding and maintaining your personal network; Community building among tech-savvy users

Twitter is touted as a microblogging tool, and, at a 140-character limit to text-based posts, the description is apt. One- to two-sentence updates, called "tweets," are submitted to the site via Short Message Service (SMS), a communications exchange protocol. The tool allows users to stay "hyperconnected" to one another and has a fiercely dedicated following, with some users submitting dozens of tweets on a daily basis. Corporations, including Cisco Systems and Whole Food Markets, use the tool to provide product and service information, and NASA used the system to announce the discovery of ice on Mars by the Phoenix Mars Lander.

LinkedIn

www.linkedin.com

Number of users: 25 million

Founded: 2003

Primary audience: Business professionals and entrepreneurs

Best used for: Expanding and maintaining your professional network; Business research and recommendations

LinkedIn is a targeted social networking site that concentrates on experienced business professionals. Where other sites emphasize personal interests, LinkedIn stresses business-related features on its profiles, including a detailed work and education history as well as the ability to provide and receive professional recommendations. According to a blog post by Guy Kawasaki on the site's official blog, LinkedIn can be used to "increase your visibility; improve your connectability; improve your Google PageRank; enhance your search engine results; perform blind, "reverse," and company reference checks; increase the relevancy of your job search; make your interview go smoother; gauge the health of a company; gauge the health of an industry; and track startups." For many business professionals, LinkedIn is the starting point for getting onto social networks. If you want more information go to: http://en.wikipedia.org/wiki/social_network_service, or go to www.wikipedia.com and type in "social networking."

LOGGING ON AND BUILDING BRIDGES

The vast amount of social networks available online may seem daunting at first glance; it's not really, though. Just take a look at your TV to see the same concept at work. At the top of the channel pyramid, you have your big networks—ABC, CBS, NBC—which have the greatest overall reach across audiences. In the world of social networking, these channels equate to MySpace and Facebook. The same way that NBC reaches specific audiences through particular shows and time slots, Facebook users are best targeted using specific groups and applications. Below the top-level networks, you have your basic cable networks—TBS, USA, and the like—which have a similar kind of generalized audience but a somewhat smaller reach. Online, these equate to smaller generalized social networks, including Orkut, Bebo, and Twitter—networks that have a widespread audience but are still no match for the large-scale networks above them. At the bottom of the pyramid, you have very specialized networks whose reach may not be spectacular, but who boast advertising-friendly targeted audiences. On TV, these are your SciFi Networks and PAXs. Online, these equate to sites like CafeMom (a network specifically geared toward mothers), Flixster (a site based on users' movie preferences), and myChurch (an online community of Christian churchgoers).

Early adopters may be saying that sites like MySpace and Facebook are "over," but in truth billions of people are just beginning to discover the influence and opportunities of social networking. For every early adopter lamenting the end of their favorite application, there are a dozen new users ready to log on for the first time. Just as some hailed the early 2000s as the end of MTV only to find that an audience shift would propel shows directly back into that epicenter of pop culture, the wave of influential users on social networks has yet to crest.

When choosing which social network to spend your time with, consider what your goals are, how much time you want to spend online, and just how much you plan to engage with the tools. Are you looking to build a new network of clients or just to keep up with friends? Do you want to show your personal network what you're doing on a day-to-day basis or do you only want to check in once a week? Base your decision on your predicted level of engagement and take it from there. Keep in mind that being on one social network does not, by any means, preclude logging on to others. Start with a single network to get your feet wet and then remember the words of Tara Hunt: "Just get out there as much as you can and build bridges." Once you've decided on your personal level of commitment, get out there and start building bridges of your own. As you develop your personal brand, you will become the very bridge you aspire to create.

FIRST THEY WERE GRADE SCHOOL FRIENDS. THEN THEY BUILT A COMPANY TOGETHER. EVENTUALLY, THEY BECAME MILLIONAIRES, THANKS TO A LITTLE HELP FROM THEIR FRIENDS. THEIR LINKEDIN FRIENDS, THAT IS.

CHAPTER 3
MAKING SOCIAL NETWORKS
WORK FOR YOU

In 2005, Eric Marcoullier and Todd Sampson founded MyBlogLog, a social networking tool for the blogging set that enables users to keep track of what blogs they've been reading and to find out who's been reading theirs. Scott Rafer, former president and CEO of popular blog search engine Feedster, was searching for a new socially based Internet opportunity and kept on running across MyBlogLog's tools in the process. Recognizing the potential of the company's offering, Rafer went online and located Marcoullier's business profile, where he then discovered a shared connection.

"I reached out to them through LinkedIn, got acquainted, and within eight weeks after doing that first search, I was CEO," Rafer recalls.

A few months later, the new CEO of MyBlogLog was at an industry conference when he was approached by a representative of Internet giant Yahoo!, who expressed interest in extending the MyBlogLog capabilities to their user base. Less than three weeks after that conference—and less than two years since the company was started—a signed contract confirmed the sale of startup MyBlogLog to Yahoo! for more than $10 million.

Bradley Horowitz, vice president of product strategy at Yahoo!, described one of the main benefits of an alliance with MyBlogLog: "This closes the loop between readers and publishers. Every publisher wants to know its readers, and the readers want to find out about each other. It's the power of implicit networking."

As for MyBlogLog, Yahoo!'s acquisition brought far more than just financial gains. In the words of Rafer: "More resources, great brand, and more process. A huge net gain."

MyBlogLog cofounder Eric Marcoullier, in a blog post discussing the just-announced acquisition, pointed to Rafer for helping to power the company's rapid growth: "We owe so much of this to [Scott], for becoming passionate about MyBlogLog and posting about us, building widgets on top of our service, and just taking time out of [his] busy life to connect with other people on [his] favorite sites and blogs."

The LinkedIn-facilitated introduction of Scott Rafer to MyBlogLog's founders is one of the first big stories to illustrate how a social network was able to push a company into the limelight of acquisition, but it is a story that is likely to be repeated as the tools spread and users everywhere log on in ever-increasing numbers. According to Rafer, "I am a big LinkedIn user because most of my job is making connections. I'm searching LinkedIn about once every working hour... the only thing I search more is Google." With big players like Rafer actively scouting on social networks, having an online presence could mean the difference between making it big and missing the train.

MANAGING YOUR ONLINE PERSONA

So, now that you know about the different social networks and just what they can do, how do you get started and what can you do to become the next MyBlogLog?

THERE IS NO VALUE IN FRIEND COLLECTING, BUT
THERE IS A MASSIVE VALUE IN BUILDING YOUR
NETWORK... IF THE END GOAL IS TO PUT GREEN IN
YOUR POCKET, DON'T FRIEND COLLECT, BUILD A
NETWORK.
—LANI ANGLIN-ROSALES

The first step to succeeding in the realm of social networks is
to get out there and create an online presence, and that means
logging on and creating your profile. LinkedIn is currently the
main platform for online business networking, just be aware
that it lacks a personal touch. As renowned sociologist Clay
Shirky points out, "Curiously, once the technology gets boring,
the social effects get interesting." Chances are you'll want to
make it more interesting by creating a profile on Facebook to
extend your reach and get the best of both worlds. You're likely
to be surprised when you first register and discover just how
many of your friends and colleagues are already using one or
both of the networks.

When it comes to filling in your profile, keep in mind that it's
best to err on the side of caution, at least at first. You may fear
that your online and offline personas will clash in unknown and
detrimental ways—and with good reason—the two should be
complementary, each reinforcing the other. What you wouldn't
say in front of your boss or your grandmother probably
shouldn't go in your profile either. Likewise, if there's an article
or blog posting that you want to show to your colleagues, why
not just post it to your profile instead? Explore as many other
profiles as you can to understand how the tools are being used
by different people and to figure out how you want to use them

yourself. Keep in mind that your profile is a work in progress and not a one-shot project. The more time you spend exploring first, the more comfortable you'll feel adding more information and a greater level of detail. Start simply and build up as you go along.

Using LinkedIn to Maintain and Grow Your Business Network

LinkedIn allows its users to post a detailed "work and education" history, and in that is quite similar to an Internet-enabled resume. Indeed, much of the information on your resume can be transferred over directly when you first create your profile. Once your experience has been posted, round out your profile by adding a detailed summary of your current work status, listing any Web sites you've helped create or operate, and providing a list of your relevant interests (keeping in mind key words that might be used to find them in a search).

The networking features of LinkedIn are where the real advantages of the site lie. They provide several opportunities to not only maintain, but also to strengthen and grow your professional network. However, keep in mind that "cold calling" is strictly frowned on; you should not attempt to connect with strangers any more than you would stand outside an office building handing out your business card. Reaching out to new connections is fine; just make sure you have a concrete reason and have specific individuals in mind before you do so. LinkedIn also provides an active hiring board that may help you find your next big job or your next star employee.

You can further increase your visibility and reach on LinkedIn by exploring and joining relevant groups, as well as by spending some time answering questions in your areas of expertise or asking some of your own. Increase credibility by providing recommendations and asking trusted colleagues to do the same for you. Remember that outdated information is irrelevant and possibly detrimental; be sure to keep yourself apprised of what people in your network are doing in addition to keeping your own activities up to date. An inactive profile is about as relevant as a month-old newspaper, whereas an actively maintained profile will keep you and your network informed and has the potential to open the doors to some never-before-possible opportunities.

Thanks to its transparency and its capacity to facilitate personalized introductions, a social network like LinkedIn can be seen as an enormous database of your community, and some of those community members are future partners, customers, suppliers, or employees. These kinds of networks empower companies to go well beyond mining for prospects and talent by allowing for detailed cross-referencing of an applicant's background, skill set, and reputation whether locally, nationally, or internationally. By the same token, the same tools that allow you to go out and search for new people also allow them to go out and find you.

Making the Most of Facebook

While LinkedIn is interested in what you worked on last year, Facebook is more interested in where you're going this afternoon. It focuses on ongoing activities, and the redesigned site puts actionable updates—such as renewing your status, posting a photo, or sharing a link—front and center on your profile.

When you log on to Facebook for the first time, you may feel a bit overwhelmed by the amount of information reflected there. The good news is that after going through a brief learning and adaptation curve, you'll find that it actually simplifies interactions and is a far more efficient way of managing your network of friends, colleagues, and acquaintances.

Using Facebook isn't as cut and dried as LinkedIn, and doing it effectively takes a bit more finesse. It's important to explore as many other profiles as you can to really get an idea of how you want to approach your own. Some key features of the site and their recommended uses follow, but ultimately it's up to you to find and create your own authentic voice.

Status Updates: Updating your status on Facebook involves posting a one- or two-sentence description of what you're up to or what's on your mind. Your name is the subject of the update and tends to be followed by an action verb (for example, Juliette Powell signed a contract!). These one-liners are the first thing people see on your profile and represent a new and unprecedented form of communication. From down-to-earth descriptions (Pebbles Mayer *is working all night to meet her deadline.*) to announcements (Marcelle Lapierre *is moving to New York!*) to questions (Michael Leatham's *in Montreal tonight. Does anybody know of any great restaurants?*) to industry-specific declarations (Ginger-Lei *loves media meshing.*), status updates are as original as the people who create them. When creating your updates, try to distill the most interesting parts of your life into a one- to two-sentence update. The more interesting you're perceived to be, the more likely you are to receive inquiries about what you've posted as well as carry influence among your friends and across your network.

Posting Items and Sharing Links: Facebook provides the ability to upload and post photos, videos, and notes, and share links directly on your profile. Posting photos or videos of you and your friends having a great time at interesting and well-attended events goes a long way toward increasing your level of influence. The same goes for photos of you together with well-known luminaries and industry celebrities. Notes are a great way to get out information or blog entries, and sharing links on your profile is becoming a widely accepted alternative to forwarding them via e-mail. Whatever you post, make sure it's something your friends are likely to find interesting and, if you receive comments, follow up with a response of your own.

The Wall: The wall, like the status update, represents a new and unprecedented contact method that is changing the way we communicate with one another. The wall is the most prominent feature of a profile and displays all recent comments and activities. Messages can be posted to the wall by you or anybody in your network. They tend to be about the same length as status updates and are viewable by anybody who has access to view the user's full profile. Private messages or longer messages bypass the wall and are instead communicated directly to the user via Facebook's built-in messaging system.

News Feed and Mini-Feed: The way to keep track of the
updates being made by you and your network is through
Facebook's News Feed and Mini-Feed. According to Facebook:

> News Feed highlights what's happening in your social
> circles on Facebook. It updates a personalized list of
> news stories throughout the day… so you'll get the latest
> headlines generated by the activity of your friends and
> social groups… Mini-Feed is similar, except that it centers
> around one person. Each person's Mini-Feed shows what
> has changed recently in his or her profile and what content
> (notes, photos, etc.) he or she has added… if there are any
> stories you don't like, you can remove them from your
> profile. News Feed and Mini-Feed are a different way of
> looking at the news about your friends, but they do not give
> out information that wasn't already visible. Your privacy
> settings remain the same—the people who couldn't see
> your info before still can't see it now.

Applications: While the vast majority of Facebook
applications are strictly for fun and have little to no
relevancy, there are some incredibly useful ones that facilitate
introductions and can help you make better use of your
personal network. Applications such as the Interactive Friends
Graph, Socialistics, and Six Degrees of Separation create
visualizations that show you all of your friends and how they're
interconnected. They narrow the playing field by highlighting
members who might be like you, live near you, work in the
same industry, or have similar tastes and interests to yours.
Everyone has something in common with one another; any
small group of people sharing a cup of coffee can have an

interesting conversation. The trick is to use technology to maximize your ability to hone in on people who might be helpful to your interests and business needs. Introduction applications on Facebook are tools that give people permission to reach out to one another and to find specific types of interactions Software developers are continually churning out new and useful applications, and you can count on new and better options becoming available as the network continues to grow in popularity.

Taking It with You: Mobile Applications

Nowadays you can do it on the street, at the airport, in the post office—new social networking applications for mobile devices mean you're no longer tethered to your computer to check in with and update your network. Facebook has an application available for multiple phones including the BlackBerry and iPhone, while LinkedIn has an iPhone-friendly application and a BlackBerry-friendly mobile site (with a full application currently in the works). The Facebook app allows you to check on your friends' status updates and to update your own—a handy feature when you're on the go—as well as upload mobile photos, add new friends, write on walls, and send messages. The LinkedIn app lets you search and research profiles, invite new connections, and receive updates on activity within your own network. Both networks offer mobile-friendly sites that provide access to profiles along with many other features.

The microblogging tool Twitter takes mobility one step further and revolves around SMS-based status updates. Twitter users often use the tool to connect with people in their vicinity in real-time, and it has been hailed as a social justice tool for its ability to break news faster than any other outlet. It essentially takes the status updates of Facebook one step further for the hyperconnected set. Most users of Twitter are on it throughout the day.

KEEPING YOUR PRIVACY

There is no better way to understand the power and the business potential of social networks than to see them in action first hand. Get your feet wet and give it a try. As a user, it is fascinating to observe how adding an event to your calendar can prompt others to do the same. The more friends you have on your list, the more people you can monitor. As more and more peers RSVP to the event, the more those observing the interaction want to join in; the herd effect gets compounded.

Imagine using technology like the Mini-Feed and News Feed to monitor your community for business purposes. What strategy would you come up with if you could see on a moment-by-moment basis who or what within your community has an immediate effect on your customer base—and who has no effect at all? What if you could track and analyze the interactions within the group and empower its influential social leaders? What if you could offer value to your community in a way that brings members and their friends coming back for more?

The ability to update your network on the go gives you an even greater level of control and lets you stay in touch no matter where you are. Just as we've gotten used to first being able to call and then e-mail people on the go, these days we check in on their status and update our own. You'll see it in action the first time you're standing in line at the bank and find yourself writing on a friend's wall.

When it comes to privacy, spend some time carefully editing the settings on each of the networks you use. You'll probably want to keep your profile closed to anybody outside your network to avoid prying eyes. You can also control the amount of information viewable by people within your network, restricting certain users to only see pertinent details. Whatever you choose to include on your profile, remember that there will always be somebody within your network who will be able to see it. Don't use social networks to post anything you want to keep private; use more traditional methods when it comes to communicating sensitive information. Just use common sense and remember that social networks are all about communicating, and, as with any method of communication, that means keeping some things private and making other things public. The real interest in social networking lies not in what you choose to hide but what you choose to display.

WHEN NINTENDO
INTRODUCED ITS WII
VIDEO GAME CONSOLE
IN 2006, IT WAS BANKING
ON NEW TECHNOLOGY
AND A UNIQUE INTERFACE
TO SHIFT THE TIDES OF
THE TRADITIONAL "MORE
PROCESSING POWER =
BETTER GAMES" IDEAL OF
THE GAMING INDUSTRY.
WHILE NINTENDO WAS

CHAPTER 4
**THE STRENGTH OF THE
MICROCELEBRITY**

challenging the gamers' idea of what makes a system worth playing, a graduate student from Carnegie Mellon University was using the same system to challenge the public's notion of what makes somebody an expert.

Johnny Chung Lee spends his days working on, as he puts it, "creating enabling techniques that can significantly increase the accessibility of technology." In 2007, Lee began working with Nintendo's popular Wii system and with its remote controller, the Wiimote. He soon discovered that the $40 controller could be hacked and repurposed to create low-cost, high-technology devices that could be made at home and that rivaled competitors 100 times as expensive. As Lee created each new device, he uploaded the accompanying software and blueprints to his Web site for free download and posted videos of himself demonstrating the projects to video-sharing site YouTube. Within a few days of posting the videos, responses were already being posted showing teachers making use of his $40 whiteboard creation and developers working with his $52 head-tracking 3D display.

It would take less than a year for Lee's YouTube Channel to attract more than 10 million views and nearly 10,000 subscribers. As his visibility rose, so did his credibility and expertise. The online gaming community embraced Lee as an everyman hero and began tracking and hailing his every move. Praise given by users of Digg, a popular social bookmarking site where Lee's videos reached immediate popularity, go a long way toward demonstrating just how much respect he was garnering online:

"THIS GUY IS QUICKLY BECOMING ONE OF MY FAVORITE PEOPLE ON THE WEB. IT IS REFRESHING HOW HE IS WILLING TO SHARE INFORMATION. A TRUE GOOD GEEK."—LCOLLADO

"DEAR NINTENDO: PLEASE, PLEASE HIRE JOHNNY! HE WOULD NOT ONLY BE A TREMENDOUS ASSET TO YOUR COMPANY BUT AN INCREDIBLE ADDITION TO THE GAMING INDUSTRY."—SKALDICPOET9

"THIS GUY IS SERIOUSLY MY NEW HERO. ALL HIS STUFF IS AMAZING, AND HE JUST SEEMS LIKE A REALLY NICE, FRIENDLY GUY."—HOOGS

Lee's videos would also catch the attention of TED conference organizers, who invited him to come demonstrate his Wiimote hacks at the 2008 conference. A video posted to the TED Web site a few weeks later shows an anxious Lee humbly thanking the audience after his demonstration garnered a standing ovation. Less than one year since he posted his first Wiimote hack video to YouTube, the graduate student turned Internet superstar's demonstration rose to become one of the Top 10 TEDtalks online.

INTERNET FAME AND INFLUENCE

As Johnny Lee found out when dozens of bloggers started appealing to Nintendo's hiring board on his behalf, more people than ever before are having experiences that were once strictly reserved for celebrities and elite socialites. It's the phenomenon of microcelebrity, and you know it's happening when complete strangers talk about you as if they personally knew you. So how do you get into that position, and what do you do once you're there?

It isn't about the power of the brand. It's about the Power of Information!

By posting explanations of his work to the Web at large, Johnny Lee eliminated the middleman and brought his work directly to his audience. More importantly, Lee was following one of the unspoken rules of the Internet: Information is worth more when it's free. In a world where cross-referencing multiple resources is as easy as performing an Internet search, people are less and less willing to pay for information, no matter how specialized or difficult to obtain it is. Lee's rise to microcelebrity built on this concept—not only did he provide free video demonstrations of his work, he also gave away the blueprints and software required to enact it.

If you've ever tried to show a child how to put something together only to be told, "No, let me do it," you've experienced firsthand the lure of personal problem-solving. It's one thing to have somebody give you a finished product; it's something else entirely to finish it yourself. Lee's videos used this idea by empowering his audience to execute and improve on his ideas themselves. When people are exposed to new ideas and given the chance to own them and share them, there's a ripple effect that happens because they are finding real value. Individuals who feel a sense of ownership are incredibly willing to get out there and promote it, even if the original idea wasn't theirs.

Nobody understands this concept better than my friend Jimmy Wales, another Internet microcelebrity and founder of the online peer-produced encyclopedia Wikipedia. Launched in 2001 as a collaborative peer-reviewed information database, Wikipedia has since developed a fierce following of self-selected evangelists.

Charismatic and energetic, site founder Jimmy Wales still sports the same trademark beard that draws attention to his piercing blue-grey eyes. Always quick to laugh, charming, and well versed in the art of the sound bite, Jimmy has become a hero for the everyman and a microcelebrity unto himself. You might expect that a man who is asked to guest lecture all over the planet and has been featured on the cover of countless magazines and in numerous news stories would pull out all the stops to set up his latest company Wikia, a free Web hosting service for wikis that enables anyone who accesses it to contribute or modify content created by both online and offline communities. Instead, Jimmy opted for a no-frills, no-fuss attitude and prefers to work out of a stark room with eight other guys in a dreary midtown New York office building to focus on the job at hand. Don't be fooled by his humble surroundings though—Jimmy knows the exact value of being a microcelebrity when it comes to growing his new company.

"Thanks to the attention I get, we are able to attract amazing people. It's not so much that they want to work with me; they know that other amazing people will come on board, and they want to work with each other. I'm just sort of the center that draws them in." This key benefit of microcelebrity ties back to being at the center of the universe for your industry—being at the center of the information flow inevitably gives you a competitive advantage.

Another factor of a microcelebrity's impact on business is that the more respected and visible you are, the more your projects automatically draw curiosity from the press and fans alike. That awareness means that when people like Jimmy talk about new developments, there's always an audience ready to listen. As he puts it, "Because people know my work and my personal brand, it's credible. We are actually going to have a large coalition form a community, and we're going to build this thing in the right way and pull this off. People know that I can do that. It's not just the technical competency of the team or the social competency of the community, which are really good. It's also that we can get attention, and that is something you need to attract a large community. You can't have community without people."

With all that attention, microcelebrities are given a public voice seemingly overnight, one that few have ever had before. Take for example a recent conference Jimmy attended in Thailand where he took the opportunity to speak out against Internet censorship in that country. The next morning, he found his appeal all over the front page of the Thai national newspaper.

"People wrote to me and said, 'Thank you so much! It's great
that someone came out and spoke out against this,'" he recalls.
"Wow! I would have said it ten years ago and no one would have
cared. So that's important—I can actually say things that I care
about and there's an audience for it. And that's, of course, a big
responsibility. You have to be very measured, because you really
can hurt people."

So, how do you wield your newfound powers responsibly?
Remember to keep your ego in check and your eye on the prize.
As Jimmy puts it:

> That's another quirk about this—if somebody wants to
> know my opinion about freedom of speech and peer-
> produced knowledge products, that's perfectly valid
> because it's something I know about and have expertise in.
> If somebody wants to know my opinion on what should
> happen next in the Israel and Palestine conflict, that's just
> ridiculous. I do restrict myself from certain topics. I just
> don't speak about them publicly. The primary reason is that
> it doesn't have anything to do with my work. It's irrelevant
> to what I do. It would be a terrible thing if people turned
> away from my work because they didn't agree with my
> opinion on something. Freedom of speech is part of my
> work. It's part of who I am and what I'm about. It's part of
> the message I want to bring to the world, in that freedom
> of speech is important for knowledge sharing and all the
> things that I care about, whereas things like McCain vs.
> Obama have nothing to do with my work so there's no
> reason for me to get involved in a public way and say here's
> why I like or don't like some politician.

THE NEW COOL KIDS

Think back to high school and to the coolest kids in your class. Remember how the popular kids seemed to have all the power? And remember how those kids could set the style for the whole school? If Jenny came in wearing spandex and suspenders, it didn't really matter how ridiculous they actually looked—her credibility alone could carry the trend. The same concept of social influence is still at work today, as Johnny Lee and Jimmy Wales will be glad to tell you. Of course, you don't have to be an Internet phenomenon to carry credibility and influence within your immediate network of friends and colleagues.

Social influencers—another version of the microcelebrity— seem to be tirelessly on the scene. They know who they are and they tend to be very entertaining. They're full of passion for what they do, they care about others, and they really work to help others get ahead. For those altruistic reasons, they're viewed as being genuine and tend to carry a lot of clout. Where the cool kids in high school exercised peer pressure and bullying to help them get their way, online social influencers demonstrate their influence in a far more genuine manner. The message they're sending to their social group, without ever having to say so explicitly, lies in the great photos of themselves and their fun-looking friends at exclusive events. Social networks simply provide the window through which to view what the influencers in your social circle are up to.

Putting yourself in the position of microcelebrity within your own network increases your own influence in easily viewable ways. You'll see it when you RSVP to an event on Facebook and immediately find your other friends RSVPing to the same one. You'll see it when you post a photo of yourself and see your friends making comments about it. You'll see it when your friends' status updates mimic or comment on your own. If you stick with it, over time, you'll see yourself slowly moving toward the center of your universe and into a position at the center of the information flow. As we've seen before, information is power—and social networks are giving the influencers and microcelebrities a lot of it these days.

YOU'D ASSUME THAT AS THE SON OF OWNERS OF A SMALL MOM-AND-POP WINE SHOP IN NEW JERSEY, GARY VAYNERCHUK WOULD HAVE STARTED TASTING WINE AT AN EARLY AGE, IF ONLY TO BETTER UNDERSTAND THE FINE DISTINCTION FROM VINEYARD TO VINEYARD. GARY'S PARENTS,

CHAPTER 5

THE NEED FOR AUTHENTICITY

however, didn't see it that way. They insisted he refrain from drinking until he was of legal age. So, instead, Gary learned the family business from the ground up—literally. In the schoolyard, Gary educated his palate to discern the nuances in his beloved wine by tasting the very elements that give wines their unique qualities: dirt, grass, and rocks.

From the beginning, Gary saw things a little differently from traditional wine connoisseurs and soon realized he could use this difference to stand above the crowd. Instead of trying to fit into the often elitist world of the wine industry, Gary decided to find his own niche. He learned early on that he wasn't the only down-to-earth wine lover out there. His customers always came to him for recommendations and appreciated his "real" approach, but he was hard-pressed to figure out how his authenticity could help grow his family's business. One day, Gary decided he could attract more people to the store by starting a small wine club after hours, a club where customers could hang out, taste his latest wine shipment, and talk sports after work. Sure enough his idea blossomed, and as time passed, more and more people starting showing up until his parents' little store just couldn't accommodate the demand. Never short on ideas, Gary pulled out his little video camera, planted it on his worktable, and started a live video blog (vlog). In short order, the overflow of Gary's fans began to watch his weekly recommendations online and purchase wine through his Web site.

Gary had leveraged his position at the center of his universe to increase his status to that of a microcelebrity. He recognized that the best way to reach a growing number of friends, clients, and acquaintances would be to create a community platform where he would be at the center of the flow of information. Nonetheless, in his quest to gain greater reach and a better position of influence, he refused to compromise who he was. Internet or no Internet, Gary was committed to maintaining his informal, playful, and irreverent approach to wine. He just needed the right social tools to amplify it into the culture.

"I didn't blog from 2001–2004 because I can't write," Gary recalls. "I stayed away from it like the black plague, even though I knew that the next wave of celebrity would come from there. I know myself, and I knew I wouldn't stick to it and couldn't execute. But as soon as that camera came, I knew it was time for me because, in that visual world, I could win! I knew myself and until I could be true to myself, I stayed away. Know thyself and harp on your strengths."

Early on, Gary decided to do the right thing, no matter what. If he was to be the man he wanted to be, he'd have to take a stand. After all, he was now wearing two hats: He was running a retail company as well as reviewing the products his company sold. To avoid a perceived conflict of interest, it was imperative to maintain integrity and be honest. When he reviewed a wine he didn't like, he made it a point to say so, even when it was a big seller that his Wine Library store had just stocked up on. The line he walked went a long way toward establishing him as a credible resource. Here was a guy who could talk sports and wine with the best of them. When he gave you his opinion on either, you just knew he was giving it to you straight.

"Doing the right thing is the whole game when you are building a brand," insists Gary. "If you want to change your life, and you don't want to be in a 9 to 5 job, start with a video blog about your hobby. Even if your hobby is watching TV, just talk about TV. How easy would it be to film yourself with a handy cam commenting on TV shows? If you're really committed to changing your life, talk about the thing you love to help you through the times when you're exhausted and want to give up."

BRINGING YOUR IDENTITY ONLINE: GARY'S WINNING STRATEGY

True to his beliefs, Gary tirelessly began building his brand equity. First he set himself an ambitious goal: He wanted to create a brand so strong that it would allow him the financial luxury of buying a sports team, complete with private jet to shuttle the team from city to city. Now who in the world would believe that an unknown guy from New Jersey could really accomplish such an imposingly high objective with a little video blog? Gary did, and for all intents and purposes, that's all that really matters. With his lofty goal in mind, Gary was targeting success, and he had a strategy. He focused on building his personal brand to help grow his business.

IDEAS ARE RAW MATERIALS. TAKE THEM! USE THEM! IDEAS ARE THE NUCLEUS AROUND WHICH CONVERSATIONS AND COLLABORATIONS FORM.
—JUNE COHEN, TED CONFERENCE

Gary locked himself in the back room of his shop every day to record a daily 20-minute video blog about his latest wine pick—and that was just the beginning. The next eight or nine hours of his day was spent uploading his latest clip to video-sharing sites and social networks, making sure he chose fun titles and tags that would attract attention and be more likely to be found on search engines such as Google. Gary reasoned that different people have different triggers, and if he could think up multiple ways to describe the content of his videos, more people would be likely to find him on a search engine. Marketing people would call that search engine optimization, or SEO. To Gary, it was just common sense.

Determined to succeed, Gary knew that if content is King, distribution is Queen, and marketing, along with business development, are the Aces in the hole. So every single day, he diligently participated in online wine forums and commented on other people's popular wine blogs, all the while embedding his Web site address in his signature so that others could track back and find his video blog. "Brands are spending $40,000 per ad to promote themselves. With social media, the tools are free. Time is your real price tag."

With a daily show and personalized responses to each of his fans' comments, 80 percent of Gary's time was spent promoting his brand, both online and off. "Chasing down your fans as well as your critics is time consuming, but extremely effective. Taking on what people say about you is more important than reading your own praise, but do read your positive feedback too. You need that praise as a motor to your success."

With little time left to concentrate on his real job, Gary
eventually delegated his duties at the family business to a full-
time staff. Gary was resolute; he would focus on spreading his
brand through community building. To that effect, he knew
he needed a hook, something he could introduce on his show
that people would want. He needed a social currency of sorts.
An avid *Star Wars* and sports fan, Gary had grown up collecting
memorabilia, trading feverishly with friends to amass his
favorites. He knew the value of *tchotchkes* and collectibles as
social currency. It all came down to figuring out what would
get his current audience's attention? His mind turned back
to sports, and he noticed that wristbands were regaining
popularity in the culture. Without hesitation, he placed an order
for 1,000 Wine Library wristbands and started wearing them on
the show. The first wristband was black. The second and third,
maroon and then the yellow wristband was introduced. From
the start, people began writing in to ask if they were for sale.
"Hell, no," was Gary's answer, "but send me your info and I'll
send some for you and your friends." And just like his beloved
baseball cards, he created the next "must have" accessory
around the Wine Library brand. Amazingly, the wristbands
worked. Fans would wear them with pride and having all the
different styles and colors meant that you had "street cred" with
other wine lovers.

Gary's personal brand skyrocketed as he became a microcelebrity, and speaking engagements started pouring in. It
wasn't long before he started to affect the culture around
him. His first prominent profile was in *New Yorker* magazine,

which then led to an article in *Time* magazine, as well as an appearance on *Late Night with Conan O'Brien*. Gary was still eating dirt and talking sports, but now he was doing it with Ellen DeGeneres in front of millions of fans who watched on from around the world. How did all that attention affect his little video blog? On any given day, Winelibrary TV (http:// tv.winelibrary.com) now has about 80,000 people watching, and viewership is growing fast.

"Meeting your community triggers emotional attachment," he says, and that understanding of how online branding initiatives need face-to-face reinforcement has gone a long way in establishing the Gary Vaynerchuk brand. Ask any social media guru who "gets it" when it comes to successfully using social networking for business, and they will direct you to Gary. He has become a poster child for demonstrating authenticity while building trust in both his personal and business brands, and has even established himself as a social maven among Fortune 500 companies.

Gary's message resonates on every video blog entry he puts out and in every personal appearance he makes: "If you want to change your life, use the gifts you were born with and position yourself to use your skills. Thanks to my natural DNA, I understand what people are thinking and how they'll react, so I use that. I'm also very good at articulating my thoughts and have a way with analogies. But that's me. Look at who you are, embrace it and amplify it."

And the monetization part of the equation you may ask: How is Gary actually making money?

"Brand equity has enormous value! If you're a brand, because you are putting out great content and you are building brand awareness, you will find money and money will find you."

Case in point: Today, wine sales all over the country fluctuate based on what Gary says as wine drinkers tirelessly watch his daily video blog.

Even more impressive is the fact that Gary's authentic personal brand, his astute social networking skills, and his nifty spittoon tricks have taken his family's business from $4 million in annual revenue all the way to $45 million. The company has seen a 22 percent growth in each of the last two years, and Gary insists that between one-half to two-thirds of that growth can be directly attributed to the success of Winelibrary TV. Truth be told, Winelibrary TV wouldn't have had any impact at all without Gary's inexhaustible community building efforts. As for Gary's personal fortune, between his paid speaking engagements and his corporate consulting gigs, Gary is well on his way to accomplishing his ultimate goal of owning his very own sports team.

So how does that happen for us mere mortals? First off, he didn't do it alone. Between the word of mouth generated by his growing fan base and his ability to surround himself with other well-known people, Gary maximized his visibility at every

step of the way. Even the guests on his show are considered
to be microcelebrities unto themselves. Take episode #499,
for example, where he talks about investing in wine with the
world-famous TV and Internet financial market commentator,
entrepreneur, and author, Jim Cramer. Put these two high-
energy guys together to talk wine and money, and you just know
that their combined viewership will explode like a Mentos and
soda experiment. Dubbed "the Internet's most passionate wine
program meets the most passionate man on TV," more than 270
comments on the episode poured into Gary's Web site within
the first few hours of its posting. Fans were elated: "Two of my
favorite personalities talking about two of my favorite things,"
wrote Jim in Atlanta. "Now this is probably my most favorite
WLTV episode. You see that wine is not just for drinking; it could
be a money maker," added user indieking, while Winelynn
enthused, "Great show, fun to watch both of you and Jim C.
was terrific as a guest. Thanks for doubling the thunder in
this episode." Indeed, doubling the thunder of two passionate
microcelebrities in an engaging online show just compounds
the fun, and the fans!

From empowering slogans like: "Because you, with a little bit of
me, are changing the wine world whether they like it or not!" to
bringing in established personalities to expand his reach and
expertise, Gary laid down the foundation for his success and
effectively put himself at the center of the action. Like a shot of
adrenaline into the arm of the very wine industry he wants to
change, the sheer momentum of Gary's microcelebrity status
projected him beyond his established social and professional
networks and into the culture at large.

BE TRUE TO YOURSELF

Gary Vaynerchuk's success relies on several factors, not least among them are his depth of knowledge and talent in sharing his passion with his audience. That being said, the point at which Gary really excels—and the point that could have made him fail just as easily—is the authenticity of his communication. In choosing to discuss wine, Gary picked a topic that he knew intimately and could truly be passionate about. Had he been less genuine, his consumers would have seen through his lack of authenticity and would have found another, more reliable source of information.

In the same way that teenagers scoff at the idea of a band that "sells out" to the whims of major record labels, savvy Internet users can see right through a corporate shill. The sheer size and breadth of the Web also means they have no shortage of places to go if they do decide to leave. Remember, once it's been lost, trust can never be fully regained.

When looking to start your own blog, vlog, or Web site, pick a topic that you not only know about, but one that you truly care about as well. Personal passion is contagious, and users will appreciate and reflect your own excitement. If you do go with corporate sponsorship and buy-ins, make sure those sponsors align with your own ideals and with the ideals of your site. In the words of Gary Vaynerchuk, "Look at who you are, embrace it, and amplify it." Be genuine and harp on your strengths— your audience will know if you don't.

SARAH LACY IS THE KIND OF REPORTER WHOSE STORIES ARE FEATURED ON THE COVER OF *BUSINESSWEEK*. KNOWLEDGEABLE, HARD HITTING, AND DIRECT, SARAH, AKA VALLEYGIRL, WAS SET TO INTERVIEW MARK ZUCKERBERG, THE 23-YEAR-OLD FOUNDER AND CEO OF FACEBOOK

CHAPTER 6
THE FEEDBACK LOOP

and one of the subjects of her book *Once You're Lucky, Twice You're Good: The Rebirth of Silicon Valley and the Rise of Web 2.0.* Her ten years as a business and technology journalist and the behind-the-scenes nature of her manuscript made her a natural to do the keynote interview at the South by Southwest Interactive (SXSWi) Festival. Nonetheless, Lacy was about to learn a hard lesson in being put on the spot, scrutinized, and belittled in a public forum.

SXSWi is home to one of the most tech-savvy audiences in the world, and the keynote interview attracted some 800 tech-preneurs ranging from bloggers and programmers to uber-geeks and digital creators who are pushing the cutting edge of technological change. So, when Mark Zuckerberg, 50 minutes into the one-hour interview and clearly irked by Lacy's unrelenting commentary and her revealing insider information, leaned over and said "I'm waiting for you to ask a question!," the audience responded with more than just a wave of laughter: They broadcast hundreds of complaints and snarky comments in real-time via mobile networking tool Twitter. Rallying behind Zuckerberg and encouraged by the camaraderie of their Twitter-based objections, the audience began to openly and unabashedly heckle Lacy.

By minute 55 of the interview, the situation had gone from bad to worse. The audience went on the attack, and Lacy responded with an astonished, "Are you laughing at me?" A resounding snicker rose from the crowd, and one audience member jeered, "Your interview sucks!" causing another ripple through the increasingly rabid crowd. In a final attempt to save face, Lacy told audience members to e-mail the reasons they felt "the interview sucked." Apparently Lacy didn't realize that as she uttered those words, hundreds of twittering thumbs were already blogging her every comment in real-time. By the end of the day, half a dozen videos of the acrid exchange had already been posted on YouTube, and hundreds more tweets and blog posts were appearing by the hour.

What happened next took everyone by surprise.

Despite the battering she had taken, that fateful—and painful—exchange boosted online pre-sales of Lacy's book that week by a factor of a thousand. In an update to her blog, Lacy noted that she was receiving "tons of positive emails, hundreds of Twitters and book pre-sales. (Also) a lot of heartfelt notes from strangers who were there and embarrassed by it."

Lacy's story is a potent reminder that if your actions are considered "different" or meaningful, you will experience a powerful amplified reaction, potentially both for the better and the worst. "My sense is, the more of a real person you are," she said, "the less people want to attack you, because ultimately everyone is human and flawed, and most people relate to that and understand that. Social networks are the tool to efficiently live as a 'brand'; they are more crucial to maintaining a brand than they are to building it. MySpace, Facebook, and Twitter are invaluable ways for me to interact with readers and viewers. I try really hard to write everyone a personal note who writes me one, but these forums give me a way to mass communicate with people too. It's an investment of my time for sure. The downside of being a brand, of course, is that it is YOU on display, not your work—no matter how much you try to make it otherwise. It is intensely personal. The measure of success is when people walk this fine line of loving you and intensely hating you, and it's very hard to deal with and understand. No matter how bad it gets, you have to be out there, you have to be polite, increasingly you have to be plastic—even as personal flaws and quirks make you more endearing to many people one-on-one."

That said, between writing bi-monthly *BusinessWeek* articles and co-hosting Yahoo's "Tech Ticker," Sarah still spends about half her time promoting her personal microcelebrity brand. Sarah's daily Web hits have shot up from a few hundred to the tens of thousands, and in her own words, "I have an amazing life. I make more money than I ever thought I would as a journalist… in the less than two years between being a *BusinessWeek* staffer and self-employed leveraging Web 2.0, my annual income has more than tripled.… If the price to pay for that is getting mass attacked a few times a year, sadly, it's just the price."

SINCERITY AND THE NATURAL ORDER OF THE ONLINE WORLD

Though Sarah Lacy was able to successfully leverage her increased visibility online, despite the negative nature of many comments, such is not always the case. In the online world, the old PR maxim of "all publicity is good publicity" is by no means a universal adage, as Web vendor PriceRitePhoto learned in 2005. Their saga began with the order of a Canon EOS digital camera from the Brooklyn-based retailer by blogger Thomas Hawk. In the days that followed, representatives from the company would repeatedly attempt to sell Hawk accessories for the camera and refuse to ship it until he agreed to purchase additional items. When Hawk threatened to write an article about the transaction, the company responded with abusive remarks, to which Hawk responded with a detailed blog post about his experience. Over the next three weeks, the story spread like wildfire through the online world and was covered in the *New York Post*, the *New York Times*, and *Fortune* magazine. PriceRitePhoto found itself flooded with e-mails, phone calls, and consumer complaints and subsequently removed from every price-aggregator and retail search engine. The online world had taken revenge swiftly and neatly, and PriceRitePhoto soon found itself out of business.

The wildfire spread of negative feedback toward PriceRitePhoto and the real-time barrage of negative Tweets experienced by Sarah Lacy expose a fundamental rule of the online world: When everything is wide open and easily accessible by the masses, you can't run, and you certainly can't hide. Different rules of engagement apply on the Internet, and revisionist history becomes simply impossible when information, once posted, leaves inerasable traces forever. You need only look at the Internet Archive's Wayback Machine, a site dedicated to archiving Web sites for cultural reference, for proof of the staying power of data on the Web. Although the wide open nature of the Internet may be an unfamiliar concept to many, it is not one to be feared. When the online world goes into attack mode, its reasons are often surprisingly altruistic, as evidenced by a blog post by PriceRitePhoto victim Thomas Hawk:

Hopefully more than anything, this story will serve as a reminder to shady businesses everywhere that in the end, fraud and abusive behavior towards customers does not pay... the power of the consumer is growing. And in a new world today with tools like blogs and social networking sites... the consumer is empowered in great ways that they never have been in the past.

Online communities do indeed feel empowered to effect change and exercise this ability whenever possible. The same principle is in operation here as was experienced by Johnny Chung Lee in the rave reception to his Wiimote hack videos. Individuals online feel a tangible sense of accomplishment when piggybacking on new and unique ideas, and they ravenously defend any concepts with which they personally identify. This principle also applies to the need for authentic communication, as demonstrated by Gary Vaynerchuk—when people are personally invested in what you're doing, they feel personally betrayed if you fail to be genuine.

So, what does all this mean for you and your business? Simply put, it means you have to be aware of and responsive to the Feedback Loop.

HOW THE FEEDBACK LOOP WORKS

When Sarah Lacy faced a seemingly unending barrage of extreme negativity at the SXSWi festival, the Twitter comment she posted upon leaving the stage reflected the same disparaging spirit she had just encountered: "Seriously screw all you guys. I did my best to ask a range of things." Once her anger was vented, Lacy demonstrated an ability to remain poised and collected as she navigated through the throngs of negative interviews and struggled to reveal her side of the story. The initial negative feedback she received was thus met and countered by her own positive feedback. In turn, her positive feedback improved the overall feedback she continued to receive thereafter. This cycle is, in essence, the Feedback Loop, and it is an unending circle.

WORD OF MOUTH IS A CULTURAL ACCELERATOR. JUST SET UP THE ARCHITECTURE TO ENGAGE AUDIENCES.
—KENNY MILLER, CREATIVE DIRECTOR & EVP, MTV NETWORK GLOBAL DIGITAL MEDIA

Gary Vaynerchuk also makes use of the power of feedback and keeps his own Feedback Loop active and flowing. He actively seeks out and responds to both positive and negative comments, ensuring that the channels of communication remain open and all commenters feel that they have a voice that is being acknowledged and responded to. Taking the time to respond to each commenter individually, in turn, makes them far more likely to continue following his work.

The old world model of feedback represented a closed, one-way street of communication, as illustrated in Figure 6.1. An event or action would occur on behalf of a company or individual, and the audience would then provide comments and feedback. Once that initial feedback was provided, the audience was left in the dark as to what effect—if any—their comments had made.

Figure 6.1

With the old model of feedback before the growth of the Internet, communication flowed only one way.

Online, the feedback cycle turns into a loop, as illustrated in Figure 6.2.

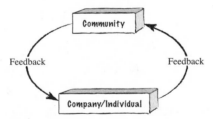

Figure 6.2

The popularity of the Internet enables communication—both positive and negative—to flow continuously from an individual or company to its community of customers and then back again.

Feedback provided by the customer community leads to a response by the company or individual who created the initial event or action. This response, in turn, leads to more community feedback. The loop continues until both parties are satisfied with the response they've received and no longer feel the need to provide feedback. It's also important to understand that if you choose not to respond to customer feedback, that doesn't turn this back into a one-way street—it simply means that your customers will continue in the loop with only their own feedback to respond to. In that scenario, the feedback has a tendency to get increasingly negative and speculative until you inject some positive feedback to change the flow. Silence in the Feedback Loop on the part of your company or personal brand could lead to negative perceptions about you and your brand. By providing feedback, you acknowledge that your community exists and has a valid opinion, and that you value them as more than just customers; you value them enough to empower them with a voice. Once empowered, your community member is far more likely to become a brand loyalist than the one who feels she has been slighted, even if the original feedback was negative. Just ask Sarah Lacy.

FEEDBACK, SOCIAL INTELLIGENCE, AND LEADERSHIP

A recently published article in the *Harvard Business Review* discusses the social and emotional intelligence wielded by effective leaders. Unsurprisingly, they discovered that the best leaders are the ones who exhibit not only influence and inspiration, but also empathy, attunement, and a genuine desire to help develop others. In conjunction with the Hay Group, the article presented a battery of questions aimed at assessing, "Are You a Socially Intelligent Leader?." Many of the questions listed proved to be a far cry from typical leadership surveys:

▶ Are you sensitive to others' needs?

▶ Are you attuned to others' moods?

▶ Do you provide feedback that people find helpful for their professional development?

▶ Do you understand social networks and know their unspoken norms?

While traditional understanding of leadership structures stressed the need for power and stern guidance, new measures of leadership are increasingly reliant on empathy and understanding. The unspoken message is clear: Be real and be compassionate. To be a truly effective leader, you need to have a team that supports you and is willing to work hard not only on your behalf, but on their own as well.

The same principles apply online. Microcelebrities like Gary Vaynerchuk and Sarah Lacy are the equivalent of socially intelligent organizational leaders. They are tuned in to their audience and keep the channels of feedback wide open, demonstrating their compassion and sincerity. Their audience trusts them and understands that even if they do make mistakes, they will own up to them through their honest feedback and reactions. That trust translates to loyalty, and loyalty builds a dedicated community.

Being accessible to your audience is only difficult when you're trying to hide something. The Feedback Loop provides you with an open and direct channel of communication with your community, and that represents a never-before-

available opportunity. Remember, the same open channel
that allows you to communicate directly with your increasingly
participatory audience also allows them to easily see through
and challenge a shill. In other words, it means that, both online
and off, honesty really is the best policy.

JEFF PULVER HAS BEEN
SITTING ON THE FLOOR
OF HIS HOTEL ROOM
FOR HOURS, STUFFING
HUNDREDS OF CLEAR
PLASTIC ZIPLOC BAGS
WITH POST-IT NOTES AND
PENS IN PREPARATION FOR
HIS FIRST EVER "SOCIAL
NETWORKING BREAKFAST."
THE BAGS ARE WHAT HE
CALLS "SOCIAL NETWORKING

CHAPTER 7
SOCIAL CAPTIAL ⇨
CULTURAL CAPITAL ⇨
FINANCIAL CAPITAL

Toolkits," and he will distribute them to hundreds of his
Facebook friends, most of whom he has never met, as they
show up to meet him for breakfast in each city where he travels
for business. The kits couldn't be simpler. Their message
couldn't be clearer: Let's take online social networking tools
offline and see what happens.

The next morning at breakfast, Jeff greets his new friends
by handing out his toolkits and inviting everyone to "tag"
themselves by writing descriptive words on the Post-it notes
and sticking them onto each other. He sets the tone by tagging
himself first: "dad," "fun-seeker," "community builder." As
the ice is broken and the tagging commences, the breakfast
time conversation revolves around social networking,
entrepreneurship, and new technology start-ups—all of which
happen to be fodder for Jeff's business investments.

Jeff Pulver has a personal social network of more than 10,000
friends. With 4,999 of them on Facebook alone, Jeff is open to
community-building and business suggestions from any one
of them. As ideas and suggestions pour in through e-mails,
comments, posts, and Facebook messages, Jeff gets to know
the suggestion-makers through their reputations online as
well as meeting them face-to-face at his breakfasts. From
there, he evaluates their submissions using a peer-based social
networking mechanism along with other more traditional
business indicators before finally choosing and retaining
the most popular proposals. The community of friends and
colleagues he has built helps him connect with, investigate, and
get to know the start-up companies he will invest in next.

Watching the flurry of activity that surrounds Jeff at his
breakfasts, an attendee sporting Post-it notes with the words
"fast talker," "funny," and "reporter" smiles to himself in the
coffee line. The community had spoken, and it was right; the
man really is a reporter, and his keen journalistic nose smells a
story in the making. In the online world, "tagging" is common.
In the offline world, this is probably a first. As a result of his
simple effort to convert online behavior to the physical world,
Jeff Pulver created a vibrant community. His social networking
breakfasts have been featured in *Fortune* magazine, and his
core business as an angel investor is thriving with more than
40 companies under his wing. Along the way, Jeff makes sure
to extend a public acknowledgement to each of his friends and
participants—not to mention, of course, breakfast.

SOCIAL CAPITAL, SWIMMING POOLS, AND SLEDDING HILLS

When you have a lot of people in your life who are willing to
support you and your ideas, people who want to hear what you
have to say and who are interested in talking *to* you and talking
about you, you are in possession of an incredible gift. That gift
is called **social capital**. If financial capital can be summarized
to mean "money," social capital can perhaps be summarized to
mean "friends," but the term actually refers to far more than the
physical individuals who comprise your personal network.

VISIBILITY AND REPUTATION AFFECT THE DECISION-MAKING PROCESS, AND AT THE END OF THE DAY, THEY INFLUENCE BEHAVIOR.

Think back to elementary school, to hot summers and no air conditioning. Now remember Suzie, that girl who had the swimming pool in her backyard. Being friends with Suzie meant being able to go swimming and to cool down on a hot summer day. Not knowing Suzie meant sweating it out in your own backyard and eagerly awaiting the arrival of autumn. Or think about snowy winter days and Mark, the boy who had a great sledding hill right behind his house. Knowing Mark meant having access to a fun winter afternoon every time school called a snow day. Knowing both Suzie *and* Mark meant you were pretty much set all year round.

The Suzies and Marks of the adult world provide access to multiple resources that come in handy at different times and in different situations. By growing and keeping in touch with a wide network of friends and acquaintances, you put yourself in the position to utilize the different and unique access points that they provide. The more Suzies and Marks you know, the more access you have to various opportunities in communication, production, and distribution.

Social capital refers to both the network of relationships you have and the access to resources provided therein. In technical terms, social capital was defined by French sociologist, ethnographer, and social anthropologist Pierre Bourdieu as "the aggregate of the actual or potential resources which are linked to possession of a durable network of more or less institutionalized relationships of mutual acquaintance and recognition." In other words, the swimming buddies and sledding pals of childhood have become the complementary business partners and high-level personal recommendations of adulthood.

For the most part, social capital is built offline and in real-time. The connections you make offline are represented online through social networking platforms that allow you to hold onto that capital for future reference and use. After you connect with a person face-to-face, the relationship requires less maintenance and can be "filed away" through tools such as Facebook and LinkedIn. Once filed, these relationships are effortlessly maintained. There is no longer a need to make the occasional call or send the occasional e-mail to make sure another person keeps your contact details. As long as you appear in each other's friends lists online, you maintain access to one another, and to one another's potential resources. Social networks are like active, self-updating, Internet-enabled rolodexes.

Most of us have movie buddies, drinking buddies, shopping friends, gym partners, and peer confidantes, all of whom make up a valuable collective of friends with different benefits. In business, we have golfing buddies, brainstorming partners, client dinners, power breakfasts, and company barbecues. With social networks, all these connections can be categorized and subcategorized into affinity, practice, interest, proximity, and so on, and these categorizations can shift fluidly depending on mood and availability. It's a different environment that has its own codified way of interacting. Social networks allow you to stay in touch with all those friends in between the golf outings and dinner meetings and to make sure they stay part of your social capital. You continue to interact through the networks so that when you do see them face-to-face, you've stayed up-to-date, and each knows what the other has been doing. The technology simply maintains the connection in between face time.

As Jeff Pulver has proven through the business suggestions he receives via his expansive network of friends, social capital is a two-way street. Not only do you have access to the resources provided by others, they have access to yours as well. In some cases, such as with Jeff, opening up access to your own resources is a powerful tool in and of itself. Jeff is able to choose and vet his next investment projects based on the people who approach *him* for resources. By opening up himself and his resources for suggestions, he eliminates the need to actively solicit proposals.

Another key element of social capital lies in access to the "weak tie." Consider your close friends and colleagues. The relationships you share with these individuals are based on multiple interactions and shared experiences, a time-tested friendship or a shared work history. These friendships and connections are considered to be "strong ties." These are also the individuals among whom you are likely to have the greatest amount of influence. The people who are closest to you—your strong ties—are far more likely to share an affinity with you, and by extension, be more motivated to be helpful to you. When it comes to social networks, it's a bit like collecting baseball cards:

It's not about how many you have; it's about which ones you have, and how you make use of them.

So what about the people you meet at a networking event and with whom you share only a conversation or a glass of wine? Here you encounter a considerably less intimate type of relationship, one that is referred to as a "weak tie" (see Figure 7.1). Perhaps, given the opportunity, these tangential relationships could flourish—yet rarely do we give ourselves the chance to find out.

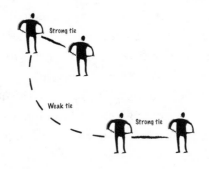

Figure 7.1
Strong ties versus weak ties.

Another form of the weak tie comes out of introductions made on social networks through trusted colleagues and friends. When it comes to online introductions, there's an implicit endorsement in the fact that one person you know is passing along a meeting, project, or deal request to one of their other contacts. There's also a qualitative aspect to having someone take the time to write a message and pass on a note on your behalf. Keeping in touch with your strong ties gives you a greater opportunity at generating new weak ties.

Social networks allow you to keep in touch with individuals with whom you share such weak ties. When you come home from a networking event with a stack of business cards in your pocket, what you've really accumulated are weak ties. Adding those weak ties to your social capital is as easy as typing in each of their names or e-mail addresses and sending an invitation to connect on a social network. Keeping in touch with weak ties means increasing your potential access to resources, which thereby increases your social capital. Social networks let you transform oft-forgotten business cards back into swimming pools and sledding hills.

CULTURAL CAPITAL AND THE MICROCELEBRITY

There was a time when social capital was all you really needed to succeed. As long as you knew a group of well-respected people who were willing to vouch for you and your company, you had it made. Nowadays, as more and more people get access to the expanded social networks of our highly mediated, interconnected society, social capital only gets you so far.

This is where cultural capital comes into play. If financial capital can be summarized as "money" and social capital can be summarized as "friends," then **cultural capital** can be summarized as "influence." Cultural capital encompasses a person's knowledge, experience, and connections, and it refers to the amount of influence and advantages a person carries in society. In other words, your cultural capital asks how much sway you carry outside your immediate circle of friends.

Take Gary Vaynerchuk, for instance. Gary started by building an audience offline and then expanded his network of friends using online initiatives such as his daily Winelibrary TV posts. This audience and network represented his social capital, but it wasn't until the wine world started making decisions based on his posts that he made the transition from social capital to cultural capital. People with a lot of social capital can influence their friends. Those with cultural capital can influence their industry and the world at large.

Or take the example of Johnny Chung Lee, the graduate student turned YouTube microcelebrity. A few months after posting his new Wiimote technology hacks, top video game developer EA announced it would be developing a hidden feature in an upcoming game based on the technology Lee created. The feature didn't make it through the final round of production, but the message was sent—Lee managed to influence the top ten developer responsible for hit games including Rock Band, Madden NFL, and Need for Speed.

In the old days, a person's cultural capital related strictly to his social standing, and that meant family, connections, and power. These days, the use of technology to reach increasingly larger numbers of highly connected people over the Internet affords every person with access and ability the chance for valuable relationships, recognition, and influence. The more adept you become at using social technology to nurture those bonds, the more you stay connected with those who want to see you succeed. If you continue building your social capital and understand the underlying dynamics of trends, feedback loops, and microcelebrities, cultural capital isn't far behind.

SOCIAL CAPITAL + CULTURAL CAPITAL ~> FINANCIAL CAPITAL

Recall the words of Tara Hunt, the Canadian expatriate who successfully used social networks to create and promote her Internet consultancy business: "I don't need a resume anymore. Just Google me." That's a pretty powerful position to be in when one is looking to leverage social capital for a good job or new clients.

When Tara began experimenting with social networks and developing an extensive network of contacts, she was building up her social capital. That same social capital came in handy when she began reaching out to clients and when starting her successful marketing blog, HorsePigCow. Her growing social capital combined with the success of both her business and her blog went a long way toward expanding her credibility and influence beyond her immediate network—that is, her cultural capital. Nowadays, Tara's credibility is immediately visible to any potential client with a Web browser. A Google search of her name brings up a multitude of interviews, videos, biographies, and conference appearances and demonstrates that Tara does, indeed, have a voice that is respected and heeded by the world outside her own social circle. That credibility translates to better projects, better jobs, and—ultimately—better financial capital.

Similarly, a Google search for Jeff Pulver brings up his sites, companies, and Wikipedia page, as well as multiple articles and interviews. When his friends submit suggestions for new companies, they already know exactly who Jeff is and what he has accomplished. His cultural capital provides instant credibility and, by providing him with greater opportunities and prospects, ultimately translates to financial capital.

When building your personal brand online, take it one step at a time. The reputation associated with cultural capital takes time to build online, no matter how well-respected your brand or company is offline. Start by building your social capital and concentrate on keeping in touch with both your strong and weak ties. Add value and build trust within your network before you try to wield your influence. Stay genuine, stay engaged, and remember to keep your ear to the ground. Opportunities within your network will undoubtedly arise, but it's up to you to find and make the most of them.

THE 2008 US PRESIDENTIAL ELECTION WAS LOOMING AND CANDIDATE BARACK OBAMA WAS IN THE PROCESS OF PULLING TOGETHER HIS CAMPAIGN BUDGET. WHILE HIS FELLOW CANDIDATES WERE RELYING ON MAJOR DONATIONS AND CONCENTRATING THEIR

CHAPTER 8

VIRALITY AND COMMUNITIES: OPPORTUNITIES IN DISTRIBUTION

advertising budgets in traditional media outlets, Obama was online mobilizing the passion and dedication of Internet users to create a fiercely devoted community of enthusiastic, if financially lacking, contributors. In short order, the seemingly paltry donations provided by his vast online community soon began adding up, and ultimately they proved significant enough to make Obama the first presidential candidate in history to bypass public financing in the general election.

The figures are truly unprecedented. Obama received contributions from more than two million donors and maintained a database of more than 450,000 backers who, according to an article in the *NY Daily News*, served as "an army of surrogate fund-raisers who [had] become his secret weapon." He managed to raise $91 million in the first two months of 2008 alone, much of it coming in the form of mere $25 and $50 contributions from his passionate online community.

The soaring triumph of Obama's online campaign, as seen in Figure 8.1, was not so much a flash in the pan as it was the culmination of a well-planned and thoroughly executed effort. A masterful web and mobile strategy along with traditional media plays—who could forget the Obama infomercial that swept across television airwaves just one week before the US election?—helped him rally ambassadors and advocates who would further spread his campaign to their own friends. Obama understood how to activate the intense passion of empowered Internet users and actively sought to build relationships with dedicated individuals, online and offline, who would serve as his own grassroots army.

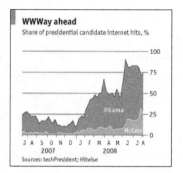

WWWay ahead
Share of presidential candidate internet hits, %

Obama

McCain

J A S O N D J F M A M J J A
   2007   2008
Sources: techPresident; Hitwise

Figure 8.1
Obama's internet hits clearly defeat McCain's.

The first presidential hopeful to make waves with his successful Internet strategy was candidate Howard Dean during the 2004 election. Though Dean grew a considerable online fan base and vowed that, "If I give a speech and the blog people don't like it, next time I change the speech," his problem lay in the gap between the Internet audience and the political center. The energy that spun out of his Internet support was never part of a larger cohesive campaign and ultimately fizzled for lack of an outlet. Dean was unable to coordinate between traditional campaigning methods on one end and the self-organizing and transparent Internet-based methods on the other. The lack of cohesion caused the overall campaign to collapse in the early phase of the election. Nonetheless, the initial success of the Web campaign offered a glimpse of things to come.

Building on Dean's strategy four years later, Obama managed to effectively connect his inner and outer political support systems to coordinate and harmonize the two circles—think of the spokes on a bike wheel connecting the hub to the outer rim (see Figure 8.2). Barack Obama captured the zeitgeist of a new era of transparent communication and was able to successfully engage with supporters at all levels. For its part, the online world found a political champion, and they continued to eagerly support his every move, all the way to the White House.

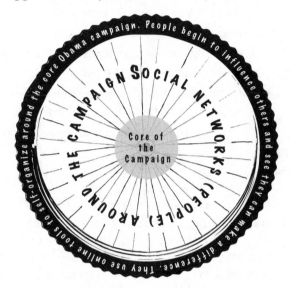

Figure 8.2
Obama's core campaign and self-organizing supporters connect and organize through social networks. Their collective efforts put Obama on the road to victory.

BUILDING A GRASSROOTS ARMY

The runaway success of Obama's Internet campaign rests primarily on three key factors, first among them a significantly larger financial investment in the online arena than those of his opponents. Obama's campaign spent 10 to 20 times more on banner ads and sponsored links than his fellow candidates, running ads across a wide array of sites ranging from large newspapers such as the *Boston Globe* to political blogs such as Daily Kos and the Drudge Report. The second key factor in the campaign's success was its lack of direct, in-your-face sales approaches. Clicking on an Obama banner ad led users

not to a donation page, but rather to a form where they could
sign up for campaign event invitations. Only *after* submitting
the form were visitors asked to make a donation. By avoiding
outright sales tactics, Obama confirmed his sincerity and sent
supporters a clear, though unspoken, message: Allegiance
is more important than money. The third factor of Obama's
campaign, and the one that would take his message from a
core group of ardently devoted followers and straight into the
general public, lay in his advisors' deep understanding of the
online world.

**MOST SOCIAL CHANGE IS DRIVEN NOT BY
INFLUENTIALS, BUT BY EASILY INFLUENCED
INDIVIDUALS INFLUENCING OTHER EASILY
INFLUENCED INDIVIDUALS.
—DUNCAN J. WATTS, PETER SHERIDAN DODDS
("INFLUENTIALS, NETWORKS, AND PUBLIC
OPINION FORMATION,"** JOURNAL OF CONSUMER
RESEARCH, **DECEMBER 2007)**

Obama's campaign understood the Internet's vast capacity for
networking and the possibilities for virally spreading a message,
as long as that message was considered meaningful, authentic,
and valuable. They also understood the value of giving people
something to believe in, and just as importantly of empowering
them to actually *do* something about it. With empowering
online mantras like: 'I'M ASKING YOU TO BELIEVE. Not just
in my ability to bring about real change in Washington... I'm
asking you to believe in yours,' Obama harnessed the power
of social networks and viral communication to connect with

the masses. And with that, the American people ushered in the world's first internet presidency.

Obama's first step was to out-organize and out-mobilize his opponents by leveraging preexisting tools on popular social networks to provide supporters with a place to gather and share opinions and comments. More than 500 Facebook groups and 100 widgets (bits of software that fans can easily embed in their profiles across popular social networking sites) formed around his campaign, most of them unofficially created by fans and supporters. Membership in the groups skyrocketed, with one group reporting more than 200,000 registered users within the first month of its creation.

Throughout his campaign, Obama comfortably led the online presidential race for popularity on MySpace and Facebook. The presidential hopeful then launched his own social network, MyBarackObama.com, which invited supporters to create a profile, blog their campaign experiences, plan and attend events, find other supporters, and help raise funds for the campaign.

Obama understood the old political system with precinct captains and ward-heelers and knew these roles could now coordinate their activities through social software and mobile applications. Even the self-organizing Facebook and Twitter groups, following Reed's Law, formed grassroots political action committees with subgroups responsible for field operations, rallies, finance, and blogs. With platforms such as MyBarackObama.com and a variety of tools across other social networking sites, Obama could further engage with people who ordinarily wouldn't go out of their way to get involved with politics in an environment that was more familiar to them.

As Todd Zeigler of the Bivings Group, a DC-based Internet communications firm that works with Republicans noted in a February 16, 2007, *Washington Post* article called "Young Voters Find Voice on Facebook": "The key point here is that the support for Obama on these social-networking sites is not being driven by the campaign itself. It is something spontaneous as opposed to something the campaign itself is orchestrating. This shows a real enthusiasm for Obama's candidacy among young people that you aren't seeing for any other candidates at this point." See page 99 for a diagram of Obama's Internet success.

"EVOLUTION" AND VIRALITY

Fat or Fab?

Wrinkled or Wonderful?

These were the questions raised by the "Campaign for Real Beauty," a marketing effort on the part of Unilever's Dove brand that prominently featured "normal" women in its ads instead of the usual, industry-standard fashion models. The campaign included everyday women with varying body types in an attempt to introduce a newly expanded view of what is considered "beautiful." As part of the campaign, a television ad titled "Evolution" first aired during the 2006 Super Bowl. The ad showed a time lapse sequence of a woman sitting down in front of a camera, being adjusted and tweaked by a multitude of makeup artists and hair stylists, being photographed in different poses, and ultimately having her neck elongated, eyes and mouth made larger, and physical proportions modified in Photoshop, with the resulting image being displayed on a billboard advertising a fake beauty product. The TV ad ended with the statement, "No wonder our perception of beauty is distorted," before directing viewers to a branded Dove site. The commercial was uploaded to YouTube immediately following its television premier. By the end of that first day, the posted video had already been viewed 40,000 times. By the end of the first month, the number of views rose to 1.7 million. By the end of the year, that number was more than 12 million.

Dove's marketing campaign, like Obama's political campaign, represents a clear case of what marketers call **virality**, or the widespread dissemination of a message that mimics a pathological virus in the way it gets passed from one node to the next. It's the biggest metric for success that people look for in a Facebook application, an online Dove ad, or a TEDtalk, and it represents the rate at which each new person introduces more than one other person to the application, video, or talk. Does the content resonate with people enough that they want to share it with their friends? The real question is, how does the "virus" actually spread?

In the words of Jon Zelner, a social epidemiologist at the University of Michigan who studies the spread and transmission of viruses, "The basic idea is this: We observe when people buy things or when people get sick, but there are many hidden variables. There is a period between when people are exposed to a disease, get infected, and when they get sick." Figure 8.3 illustrates the path of viral infection in a community during flu season.

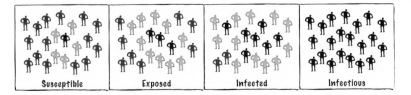

Figure 8.3

Path of a flu-based viral infection: Susceptible (It is flu season and people in my town are getting sick; therefore, I'm susceptible to getting sick too)→Exposed (My friends and work colleagues are sick)→Infected (I get sick)→Infectious (My healthy friends are exposed to my flu virus).

The same goes for product exposure, as described in Figure 8.4. The iPhone goes on the market, and everyone is talking about it. Many of your friends have iPhones and are raving about them. The period between exposure and infection is called **incubation**—somewhere in the back of your mind. You've already made the decision to buy the phone, but you have yet to actually walk into the Apple Store and put the money on the counter.

Your chance of infection (that is, how likely you are to actually go out and buy the product) increases with exposure. If only one of your friends has an iPhone, the chance of you going out and buying one based on that influence is much lower than if ten of your friends have iPhones. The higher the exposure rate, the higher the rate of infection. And if you do end up going out and buying an iPhone, you yourself now become infectious.

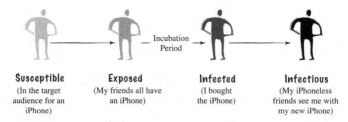

Susceptible	Exposed	Infected	Infectious
(In the target audience for an iPhone)	(My friends all have an iPhone)	(I bought the iPhone)	(My iPhoneless friends see me with my new iPhone)

Figure 8.4

Path of a product-based viral infection: Susceptible (I'm in the target audience for purchasing an iPhone)→Exposed (My friends all have iPhones)→Infected (I bought the iPhone) →Infectious (My iPhoneless friends see me with my new iPhone).

As more and more people ask, "Hey, have you seen that new Dove ad?," you eventually feel the need to go online and watch it. Similarly, as more and more of your friends become supporters of Obama '08 on Facebook, you eventually feel the need to show that you too are a supporter. Keep in mind that understanding the spread of a virus doesn't automatically translate to millions of page views or unprecedented sales. The content of the message you're sending is all-important, and that content doesn't necessarily have a direct correlation with how viral or infectious it is. Some amazing messages never spread further than the individuals who create them, and a lot of what does spread virally isn't particularly valuable. Understand the basics of virality and how an infection spreads and be sure to heed the words of *Tipping Point* author Malcolm Gladwell (as noted in a recent blog post): "Virality is more of an outcome that you hope for as opposed to a tactic in and of itself."

MOVING FROM AUDIENCE TO COMMUNITY

Like an unannounced tornado barraging through the town square, the Internet has come from seemingly out of nowhere to completely redefine our lives and the way we do everything from politics to business. The roles of content provider and consumer have become increasingly muddled, and the traditional view of the audience has been turned on its head. Where once an audience functioned strictly as a receiver— you, the provider, put out a product, and they, the audience, received and used it—the audience has now become an active participant in the feedback and creation process. It's no longer enough to talk *to* your audience. These days, you have to talk *with* them.

"Because of the impact the Internet had in the election, we're expecting to see the incoming (Obama) administration embrace a lot of those tools, and that will be important for laying the groundwork once the administration takes office," Alan Davidson, head of Google's Washington office.

The first step in engaging your audience is to find out where it lives online. Whether you've created a forum for them or not you can be sure that your community already exists in some form, though it's likely to be scattered across multiple sites and networks. Study that community to understand what's important to its members and what they do best. Understand your audience, its strengths, and the ties that exist with it.

Once you've pinpointed your community and come to understand their habits and motivations, become part of the conversation. Cater to their natural interests and talents and engage with them authentically. Share insights. The best way to stimulate meaningful and fruitful business relationships is to give your community a helping hand. There is a marked difference between cold calling people to sell something and contacting people because you see that they have a need and can recommend a solution, especially if the solution isn't perceived as self-serving. With social networking tools, your entire network is at your fingertips. How easy would it be to forward along helpful articles, topical blog posts, and other relevant information to various affinity groups within your network? What about recommending suppliers or former coworkers? All these small things make a big impression. The resulting dividends on your time investment could be exponential.

Remember, transparency and trust are key—if people perceive you're only there to make a buck, your plan is bound to backfire. Experiment with free, preexisting tools in widely available networks such as Facebook and YouTube to understand your best approach to creating a viable and authentic community. And remember that you cannot force people's behavior. What you can do is

- ▶ Look at the underlying dynamics of the way people interact with each other and with your brand.

- ▶ Identify and understand the patterns of interaction: Who is influencing the larger group to do things such as purchase products or attend events and how are they doing so?

▶ Reward social influencers in your community. Feature them on your home page and give them the company's endorsement to moderate your online network.

▶ Constantly tweak the rules of interaction to reflect changing behavioral patterns.

The very nature of social networking software makes adding value to people's lives easier than it has ever been before. As Barack Obama learned in his first presidential term, an engaged community of supporters is an extremely powerful tool and can provide a self-perpetuating support and guidance system for you and your business. "If change.gov—the new site for the President Elect—is any indication, the second act of Obama's social media strategy may have even more impact on the United States than the impressive—and historic—first act," affirms blogger Rick Turoczy. Luckily, the tools aren't only reserved for the leader of the free world, they're at your fingertips. It's up to you to leverage those tools and convert your customers from a static audience into an interactive community.

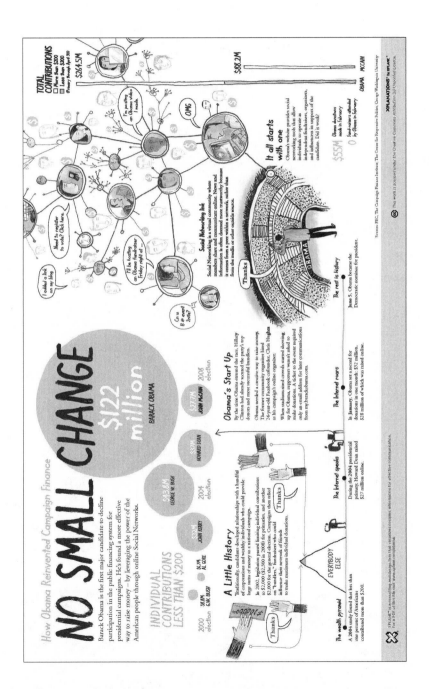

IT WAS THE HEIGHT OF
THE DOT-COM BUBBLE,
AND EVERYBODY WAS
GETTING IN ON THE GAME.
SO WHEN A COUPLE OF
COLLEGE DROPOUTS WITH
NO FORMAL BUSINESS
TRAINING GOT TOGETHER
IN 2000 WITH $500 EACH
AND DECIDED TO START A
T-SHIRT SHOP ON THE WEB,
NOBODY PAID MUCH

CHAPTER 9

**CROWDSOURCING
AND COCREATING:
OPPORTUNITIES IN
PRODUCTION**

attention. Not at first, anyway.

Jeffrey Kalmikoff and Jake Nickell got the idea for their online store from a T-shirt design contest that Jake entered and won through an online design and development community they were both part of at the time. The idea of that contest stuck, and they decided to use the same principle to build their own ongoing, community-based T-shirt design contest. Nobody expected that these two college dropouts would go on to become the multimillionaire creators of a new standard of peer production on the Internet.

"In a nutshell, our business is based upon the idea of 'customer cocreation' or 'user innovation' or 'crowdsourcing' or whatever the next buzzword for it is," muses Jeffrey Kalmikoff, cofounder and chief creative officer of online retailer Threadless. After expanding at a rate of 3 to 4 times a year and becoming one of the most popular shirt-makers on the Web, Threadless now pulls in an annual revenue of about $30 million with a profit margin clocking in at an impressive 30 percent.

As illustrated in Figure 9.1, the Threadless Crowdsourcing process goes like this. Seasoned designers and novices alike submit more than 1,000 new T-shirt designs a week to the Threadless Web site. Users then have a seven-day window in which they vote on and rate the submissions. The company finally chooses designs from the top-scoring submissions to be printed in limited quantities of 1,500. Invariably, every single design sells out.

Figure 9.1
Threadless represents a win-win-win game of peer production and crowdsourcing.

Designers whose T-shirts get printed receive $2,500 in cash and prizes, a hefty sum considering that some designs are created by amateurs with no professional design experience. The community, for its part, gets to participate in the creation process and feel the honor by association of, "Yeah, I voted for that one." The company itself never has to deal with the risk of a poorly selling shirt. By banking on preselected winners, every design is a sure thing.

When Threadless based its Web site on user-submitted creation, it was leveraging the recently emerged trend of crowdsourcing. Crowdsourcing means taking a task normally completed by a single professional—say, for instance, t-shirt design—and opening it up to contributions by a group of non-professionals. Crowdsourcing is comparatively low-cost and provides a far wider array of options to choose from when creating a product. Threadless uses crowdsourcing as the fundamental basis for its business model.

The runaway success of the online retailer led it to open its first brick-and-mortar retail store in Chicago in 2007, and it has plans to open several other locations across North America in cities including Portland, Austin, Toronto, and Boston. Threadless parent skinnyCorp also launched a sister site called Naked & Angry (a play on Threadless' slogan "Nude no more") using the same user-scored submission basis for products including neckties and wallpaper. A bevy of Threadless imitators has also come onto the scene, as have other user-submission-based store models.

"It's a simple concept," says Kalmikoff. "When people tell you what they want, you give it to them."

SOURCING THE CROWD

TODAY'S AUDIENCE ISN'T LISTENING AT ALL—IT'S PARTICIPATING. INDEED, AUDIENCE IS AS ANTIQUE A TERM AS RECORD, THE ONE ARCHAICALLY PASSIVE, THE OTHER ARCHAICALLY PHYSICAL. —WILLIAM GIBSON, AWARD-WINNING AUTHOR (EXCERPT FROM *WIRED* MAGAZINE, JULY 2005)

We live in a world where a wealth of high-quality amateur content is being produced and developed right alongside the industrial model. There is a shift in the traditional power structure whereby anyone with access to the Internet and an affinity for technology can produce and distribute a product or service that directly competes with you and your business. On-demand printing sites such as CafePress and Spreadshirt allow users to upload designs and open their own T-shirt and accessory stores completely free of cost. As Gibson noted, the audience is no longer content to stay in the role of receiver— today's audiences want, and in more and more cases expect, to directly contribute and participate.

Decreasing technology costs and the increasing ubiquity of inexpensive and specialized software have put previously inaccessible tools of professional creation directly into the hands of the consumer. Whereas once a musician needed to pay extraordinarily high fees for equipment and studio time, near professional-quality production tools such as Apple's GarageBand now come standard on new computers. The same goes for video and graphics editing software. That means more and more people are able to experiment with these once unavailable tools, and that in turn means more and more people are discovering innate talents that might otherwise go unnoticed.

Where crowdsourcing encourages participation and harnesses peer-production within a large dedicated community, it simply doesn't work if the crowd is too small. A group of 50 nonprofessional T-shirt designers is unlikely to come up with hit designs on a regular basis. If Threadless had started out expecting to select and print ten designs every week, it would have failed from the get-go. It had to start small and build not only its credibility, but also the crowd from which it sourced its designs.

What that means is, for mom-and-pop companies at least, crowdsourcing is unlikely to be a viable option. Without a vast community to use in soliciting responses, sustainable talent is a rarity. Even a novice will occasionally hit a hole-in-one on the golf course; just don't ask her to do it twice in a row. Realistically, crowdsourcing is best used in one of two ways: (1) as a one-off or (2) by larger companies, or companies with dedicated and/or talented communities.

Crowdsourcing as a One-Off

Canadian gold-mining company Goldcorp did it on a large scale when it released a unique challenge back in 2000: "We'll give you all of the data about one of our mining regions; you tell us where to dig for gold." The competition attracted entries from geologists all over the world and offered prizes worth a total of $575,000. The top prize was taken by Fractal Graphics, a small consultancy based in Perth, Australia. Fractal's prize: a cool $105,000. Goldcorp's net take from the contest data: more than $3 billion.

On the other end of the spectrum, *Wired* editor Jeff Howe used crowdsourcing to come up with the cover for the UK edition of his upcoming book on—you guessed it—crowdsourcing. More than 150 designs were submitted, and the winner received a signed first edition of the title and framed artwork along with a cash prize of £500.

As a one-off, one-time contest, crowdsourcing represents a low-cost source of high-value talent. It's the one-hit wonder of the Internet—relatively easy to hit once, incredibly difficult to achieve consistently. Social networks provide a vast source of potential talent for creating your own crowdsourced one-hit wonder. Whether creating a new product or looking for improvement on an existing offering, consider the dedication and talent of your community before paying top dollar for a specialist. If you're looking to make a better coffee machine, leverage the passion that consumers have for your product by asking them for suggestions. Build a better product by getting advice from the people who use it on a regular basis.

Crowdsourcing a Dedicated Community

The other viable option for crowdsourcing only works if you have a large and/or dedicated community—and even then, be aware that it has its risks. Crowdsourcing is best utilized when your community has a real passion for what they're creating. To create a sustainable business based on user submissions, you need to have a community that is either unusually talented, or one large enough to consistently produce high-quality submissions.

One of the most recent entries into this arena is Ryz, which runs on a similar model as Threadless but uses sneakers instead of T-shirts. Though, at the time of publishing, the site is just getting started, it has already created several successful sneaker designs and boasts consistently high-quality submissions. Ryz leveraged the current urban trend of custom-designed sneakers to attract talented designers into its submission process. Like Threadless, winning designers receive a cash prize. Unlike Threadless, the contest is not ongoing—Ryz has not yet built an expansive enough audience to keep its doors open at all times. That is likely to change as recognition spreads, and both users and buyers flock to the site in increasing numbers.

THE GIANTS OF COCREATION

Isaac Newton once humbly wrote, "If I have seen further it is by standing on the shoulders of giants." Newton understood that all new concepts are built on preexisting concepts; if he himself created new theories, it was because he was able to build on the existing theories of his predecessors. They had constructed the fundamental concepts upon which he was able to stand to see new, previously unexplored lands. In other words, they gave him the basics; he just elaborated on them.

The concept of cocreation operates similarly. It's a little like those group projects you worked on back in high school. Joe was the best writer, Jane was the best researcher, and you were the best presenter. As a group, you divided and conquered by concentrating on your strengths and then combining them to form a better whole. Rather than relying on a single individual to do all the hard work, you combined your efforts to come up with a better end product. Similarly, by separating a development project into its constituents, you can create a whole that is greater than the sum of its parts.

The term "cocreation" is often used synonymously with crowdsourcing, but the two carry different connotations. While both refer to using the wisdom and talents of a group to create a better end product, each goes about it differently. Crowdsourcing involves soliciting ideas from a wide group of people and ultimately choosing the best final product from among the submissions. Cocreation, on the other hand, asks a group of people to work *together* on creating the best final product. In crowdsourcing, each person works on the end product *individually*, and the best option wins. In cocreation, a group of people comes together, and each person concentrates on a different element, finally combining their talents to make a better collaborative solution.

Cocreation is at the heart of the open source software move-ment, where users are given full access to the programming code for a piece of software and can then submit their own changes and improvements for approval. The best example of cocreation is perhaps Mozilla's Firefox, the open source Web browser that has been slowly but steadily chipping away at the once overwhelming lead of Microsoft's Internet Explorer. Firefox bases much of its development on the input of loyal contributors who provide updates in the form of source code tweaks as well as in the form of useful plug-ins and add-ons. These self-selected developers work long hours to improve the product they love and support with as only compensation accolades from their peers and the satisfaction of a job well done.

WORKING WITH YOUR COMMUNITY

"The key to maintaining a good community is honesty," says Threadless cofounder Jeffrey Kalmikoff. "Our community is like any community. We could even give away free money and someone would complain. We make changes to the site and some people aren't happy. The key is to stay transparent and let the community know what's going on. As long as people feel like they have a sense of ownership and still have a say (which they do) in what goes on, we can do anything."

That sense of ownership is exactly what drives individuals to participate in crowdsourcing and cocreation platforms with little or no financial benefit. That sense of ownership is exactly what drives individuals to participate in crowdsourcing and cocreation platforms with little or no financial benefit. Just as Obama's cocreation strategy paved his way to the presidency, his participatory change.gov initiative and groundbreaking weekly address to the nation via Youtube is helping to shape a new form of political process. In politics as in business, the real payoff comes when eager and dedicated individuals come together and work toward an ultimate goal they can trust and believe in.

When developing your own initiatives, consider several factors before committing:

▶ Is your community dedicated enough to provide useful and significant input?

▶ Is it large enough to be able to provide unique value?

▶ Does it make sense to vet your offerings through your community before publicly releasing them?

▶ Is your community passionate enough to provide valuable insights?

▶ What are the best questions you can ask your community to generate real, tangible value?

Concepts like crowdsourcing and cocreation networks are often played down by big media outlets as ineffective and valueless, but by and large the reason for that portrayal lies in the multitude of companies that attempt to use the concepts without first taking the time to consider both the benefits and the consequences. They are concepts that, when used correctly, have the potential to provide tremendous and lasting value with a minimal investment. Do your research before jumping in, and if you decide to go for it, make sure you know exactly why and how. As always, be genuine, and if you're asking your community to give you something, make sure you have something they value to give them in return. If used correctly, crowdsourcing and cocreation represent some of the biggest potential returns on investment (ROI) out there today. As President Obama found out in his historic presidential nomination:

"Nothing can stand in the way of millions of voices calling for change!"

THE STEREO GEEKS IN ONE STORE HAD NO IDEA WHAT WAS GOING ON IN ANOTHER. HOW DID THE 6 1/2-INCH PIONEER TS-D1602R COAXIAL CAR SPEAKERS WITH KEVLAR AND BASALT WOOFER CONES COMPARE WITH THE 6 1/2-INCH SONY XS-GT1625A CAR SPEAKERS WITH HOP WOOFER CONES?

CHAPTER 10

OPENING THE CHANNELS, INSIDE AND OUT: OPPORTUNITIES IN COMMUNICATION

An important distinction, to be sure.

But when Best Buy sub-brand Geek Squad decided to roll out an internal **wiki** (a collaborative tool where anybody with access can share and modify information) to its 11,000 employees, the powers that be really had no idea what the employees were going to use it for.

The terrifying fact about investing in an internal social network and encouraging employees to use it lies in the fact that interaction within it appears to be totally random, even chaotic. Logically, you'd think it would only result in staffers playing around all day instead of doing what they're being paid to do (that is, their jobs). You'd also think that all that time spent playing around would seriously drag down productivity. But Best Buy and Geek Squad decided that, for better or for worse, they were willing to embrace the experimentation and uncertainty inherent in their new internal network. They simply rolled out their new social tools and promoted them to see what would happen next.

But contrary to what you might expect, employee productivity didn't go down after all. What did happen next was that some users started making pages about their own stores, while others made pages about customer service issues. In fact, productivity actually *increased* as more pages were added.

The pattern that then emerged is based on a seemingly obvious but nonetheless insightful observation: Specialists *love* to share their knowledge with others. For Geek Squad, this meant that

the stereo geeks who know everything there is to know about
the Pioneer stereo systems could suddenly share information
with the stereo geeks who know everything there is to know
about the Sony stereo systems. As my friend Jimmy Wales
explained to me, until the company's wiki was launched, the
opposing-brand geeks had no way to share their experiences,
let alone to get credit for that knowledge within the company
at large. Nowadays, when a Best Buy store doesn't have any
stereo geeks in it with an inherent knowledge of the latest
Pioneer subwoofer, any Best Buy employee can log on to the
company wiki to get in touch with their inner geek and find
recommendations for customers, and to educate themselves
while they're at it.

But why would Best Buy even invest in a social network in the
first place? They already represented a credible brand with
plenty of brand loyalists. Why would a well-respected brand
like Best Buy feel the need to embrace such a chaotic and
unpredictable medium? To answer that question, I turned again
to Jimmy who suggested I try and imagine how things used
to be run. In the old days, the Sony stereo geek working at the
Best Buy in New York City really had no way of getting in touch
with the Pioneer stereo geek working at the Best Buy in Palo
Alto (particularly if it was 10 a.m. EST and nobody in California
had arrived at the store yet). Truth be told, the time difference
never even came into play—the fact was that neither of the
geeks had any idea that the other even existed. The best they
could do was to tell their own manager something, hoping that
their manager would then pass that something on to another
manager. If they were really lucky, their message might then get
sent to headquarters. If they were *really* motivated, they might

even send out a report about it. In corporate reality, that kind of thing just didn't happen. Best Buy at the time had no real flow of information regarding expertise within the company. The experts were out there, but everybody was too isolated to know about it.

These days, the internal community nurtured by Best Buy and Geek Squad provides real and tangible benefits to its external customers. It also contributes to morale by giving employees the feeling that they are adding value that goes beyond the scope of their jobs. The change in the flow of information is also radical because it's completely bottom-up. It's no longer about what somebody at corporate headquarters thinks customers need to know. Now, it's all about the front-line employees who interact with customers on a daily basis. If the questions they are asked by customers aren't already in the official Best Buy customer guidebook then, most likely, headquarters won't have a clue how to answer them anyway.

Best Buy understood that their traditional hierarchical system represented a total waste of human energy. All it did was promote redundancy. If I go to a store now, I'll end up with much better information about the stereo I'm inquiring about than I ever would have before. That's because with Best Buy's new internal tools, employees are better able to educate themselves than ever before. That self-education on the part of the employee then leads to a better experience for me at the store, which in turn results in an increasingly positive association with the store brand. Just like with Threadless' peer production system, Best Buy's internal wiki represents a win-win-win *(company-store-customer)* situation.

"A VIEW FROM DEEP INSIDE THE INTESTINES OF A GLOBAL COMPANY"

**PRODUCTIVITY IS SECOND TO CONNECTION: NETWORK PRODUCTIVITY TRUMPS INDIVIDUAL PRODUCTIVITY.
—STEVE BOYD**

They were already doing it on Facebook. More than 4,000 employees had voluntarily created and joined a group on the popular social networking platform where they were connecting and discussing their employer. The problem was, their employer was nowhere to be seen. As Richard Dennison, social media chief of BT (formerly British Telecom) and key developer of the company's group knowledge management strategy, noted in a blog post: "if that's not a cry for greater collaboration, nothing is!"

Under Dennison's behest, BT would go on to become a case study in successful adoption of social media tools. BT's set of robust internal collaborative tools includes BTpedia, an enterprisewide wiki that allows employees to publish and edit articles; a blogging tool that found itself host to more than 300 blogs within the first couple weeks of its launch; and a powerful profile-based social networking tool called MyPages. It was MyPages that allowed users to create Web pages, upload photos, blog, and connect with others within the organization, and that sent adoption rates soaring almost immediately.

On his blog "Inside Out," a self-described "view from deep inside the intestines of a global company," Dennison gives some advice to companies looking to get started with social media tools of their own: "Starting out along this road on your own is pretty tough… harnessing the enthusiasm of the enthusiastic makes it a much less lonely trip. Social media is a "bottom-up" phenomena… gather together some co-conspirators and let the revolution begin!"

OPENING UP TO YOUR COMMUNITY

Both BT and Best Buy were able to successfully leverage social media tools to better facilitate internal communication between geographically and departmentally dispersed employees. That improved internal communication ultimately translates into a more effective workplace and better service for their customers. So what about using those same tools to allow your community to connect and share information with each other?

With more than 16 million subscribers and still growing, World of Warcraft (WoW) is easily one of the most tightly knit communities on the Web. And with more than 57,000 articles and also growing, the user-generated WoWWiki is your go-to place for finding out the difference between the Silverwing Sentinels of Ashenvale and the Hydraxian Waterlords of Azshara.

Now imagine if you were a company trying to produce all that content around WoW. That's a 57,000 article uphill battle. Now also imagine trying to generate content that customers like instead of making it about what someone at the office *thinks* they'll like. These types of communities don't want to be on a company-run wiki, or on a moderated social network for that matter. It takes a special kind of company to have enough trust in the community to allow them to freely voice their opinions, whatever those opinions might be. It is with that level of trust in the community that the community feels like it can openly participate. And participate they do—according to Internet ranking site Alexa, WoWWiki, part of the Wikia network, is one of the top 1,000 Web sites in the world.

On the other end of the spectrum is the official wiki for ABC's hit TV series, *Lost*. The popularity of the show is soaring, and you'd think its wiki would be one of the most popular ones on the Web. Problem is, people don't really like it; they'd rather use one of the two fan-maintained *Lost* wikis. The information on ABC's wiki just isn't as good, and users have even accused the company of censoring rants or criticism against the show or the writers. Indeed, the official wiki's FAQ reserves the right to delete posts that don't comply with its "Code of Conduct" or with ABC.com's "Terms of Use." ABC insists all feedback has to be positive and in support of the show, because that's the way network executives think the official Web site should be. The community's reaction has been predictable: "I want to write about *Lost*, but I don't want to be subject to a company's whims."

Independence is a key element for maintaining a thriving community. Without the freedom to openly express their opinions, the community will move on until they find a place where they can. And as ABC found out, there's no shortage of other options.

INSPIRING BETTER COMMUNICATION

So what do Geek Squad, BT, World of Warcraft, and ABC all have in common? For one, they all experimented with new social technology and created custom offerings for their communities, all of which—with the exception of ABC's unsuccessful *Lost* wiki—passed with flying colors. Look a little closer, and you notice that the real thread they share lies behind their use of technology and in a common decision: Let's open up our channels of communication and see where it takes us.

When deciding on how to make the best use of preexisting or custom-built social networking tools to improve communication, your best approach is to just ignore the tools—at first, anyway. Consider what you're looking to improve and what you hope to gain by inspiring improved interaction. Do you want to open up the channels of communication within the company, or do you want to provide your customers with a better way to communicate with one another? Are you looking to create a dedicated community or are you just looking for a better way to share information? Only after you've answered those questions and made your decision should you start looking at what tools are available to help you enact it.

If you're looking to improve the flow of information internally, a wiki may be for you. Before diving in, though, ask yourself whether employees are likely to even use it, and if they do, will they waste their time on it or use it productively? What information are you looking to share, and is there another way to share it?

Externally, be sure to keep the real motivations of your community in mind at all times. As Jimmy reminded me, while you see a dedicated community form around a preexisting passionate community like World of Warcraft, what you don't see is a whole wiki forming around a company like retail giant Costco. Not too many people in the world are so obsessed with Costco that they need a community to talk about it. Just because you love shopping at Costco the store, doesn't mean you're particularly interested in discussing Costco the company. Where the company stands to benefit from a social networking platform is in providing a forum to discuss the products they offer. Tie popular group discussions in with discounts at the store and suddenly customers have a reason to register and talk about their favorite products.

As always, be genuine in your offering. You can't force a conversation any more than you can force a purchase. Also, keep in mind that building tools with a specific community in mind doesn't necessarily predict who will actually use it, as US-based social network Orkut discovered when it was overtaken by users from Brazil and India. Just remember, any dedicated community is a valuable community as long as it remains active and passionate. While you cannot control who will be engaged in your online community, you can encourage those who are to keep coming back and to tell their friends. Create a system where you can engage in a dialogue with participants that allows you to distinguish between the needs of your diverse community members and remain flexible enough to listen to their recommendations and implement commonly suggested changes quickly. It's up to you to open the channels of communication. It's up to your employees and community members to do the communicating.

HE WAS VICE PRESIDENT
OF THE UNITED STATES
FOR EIGHT SUCCESSFUL
YEARS, AND FOR MANY,
THAT WOULD HAVE
BEEN ENOUGH. NOT FOR
AL GORE. YET WHEN IT
CAME TO RUNNING FOR
PRESIDENT, HE DIDN'T
QUITE MAKE IT BACK INTO
THE OVAL OFFICE. GORE
TRIED, HE LOST, AND,

CHAPTER 11
SUCCESS IS WHERE YOU
FIND IT

if novelist F. Scott Fitzgerald is to be believed, the story ends there: "There are no second acts in American lives." In Fitzgerald's era, if something went wrong in a person's chosen career, there was no second chance to start it over again. These days, second acts can and do happen. Just ask Britney Spears and Robert Downey Jr.

In the United States presidential election of 2000, Al Gore won the popular vote but ultimately, thanks to a decision handed down by the Supreme Court, lost to Republican candidate George W. Bush. The defeat was humiliating, yet through it all, Gore would learn an invaluable lesson, one that would ultimately help him to change the course of history. With the defeat of Gore the politician, Gore the man could stop thinking about how he was supposed to act and start just being himself.

Despite his election letdown, Al Gore never gave up on the idea that he really had something of value to contribute to the world. With that thought in mind, he chose to pursue a topic that he was deeply passionate about. In 2002, with the sting of failure still a little too close to home, Gore began reaching out to communities about the issue of global warming. The first of his presentations was met with a childlike taunting on the part of the media aimed at his newly grown and uncharacteristic beard. Beard or not, what Gore's audiences saw was an insightful and authentic man who put his ego on the back burner in favor of a much bigger issue.

Global warming had been a topic du jour that many Americans took with a grain of salt. Gore was able to come in and change all that by bringing the once-maligned topic straight into the public eye. A confluence of factors contributed to the success of Gore's campaign around the climate crisis, not least among them the fact that it was simply an idea whose time had come. Beyond that, the global warming issue had found a new champion; one who had learned how to use his authentic voice to leverage his expansive personal network and infuse his message into the culture at large.

After the initial success of his presentations, Gore went on to build a mechanism of broadcast and broadband distribution called Current TV. Current relied on the same grassroots community building methods that he had been hoping to tap into, and it became the vehicle by which Gore, for the first time, could finally come into his own and find his own voice. The programming format on the network was made by the people and for the people. Content consisted of stories and commercials that, echoing crowdsourcing systems like Threadless, were submitted and voted on by a dedicated online community. Gore's newly gained ability to reflect and affect the culture at large would play an important role in what would become his next major challenge.

With a little help from his friends, Gore dispensed with the same old environmental issue on the political agenda and helped rebrand it into a full-blown global climate crisis. He also empowered individuals everywhere to feel like they could actually *do* something about it. Gore willingly put himself in the center of that crisis to galvanize and captivate an eager participatory audience. That willingness went a long way toward increasing his ability to influence the world at large.

Perhaps the real key to Gore's success in creating such widespread awareness was in a combination of his ability to passionately and convincingly communicate what he knew on the one hand, and on the other, in his shrewd ability to disseminate his message through his vast personal social network as well as to the multitudes of people who knew about him. In other words, he was able to spread his message as far as he did by making use of both his social and cultural capital. Buy-in from the general population grew organically as his message spiraled out to people wherever they lived: in movie theatres, at magazine counters, and through online methods including social networking platforms and virally spread videos. Gore's hundreds of personal appearances in community centers, churches, and schools helped to further fuel that growth with countless positive feedback loops. Throughout his personal crusade, Gore successfully injected awareness and a sense of urgency into an issue that had already been on the debating table for decades. He successfully reached out to people across a variety of spectrums—Democrats and Republicans, young and old alike—galvanized them around a single idea. Al Gore himself became the creative spark of positive change.

In February 2006, a few months before the premiere of *An Inconvenient Truth*, the documentary film based on his original PowerPoint presentation, Al Gore stood in front of some of the most well-connected people in the world on the stage of a familiar Monterey auditorium. Standing before the audience gathered at that year's TED conference, Gore went through an updated version of the same climate crisis presentation that had inspired his movie. Was this funny and passionate speaker who breathed new life into a stodgy slide show presentation the same man who had been described just a few years earlier as "boring" and "annoying"? More importantly, would Gore's message be picked up and supported by the TED community?

The film's producer, Lawrence Bender, was in the audience to hear the talk and remembers that day vividly, as does June Cohen: "The TED community was incredibly influential in getting word about the movie out there. Beyond word of mouth, TEDsters donated their time, money, and free media space for the promotion of the film." TED also held two private screenings before the official theatrical release to get the feedback ball rolling. Meanwhile, the founders of Google, themselves members of TED, held several private screenings for all 10,000 of its employees. Another prominent TED member and a strong supporter of conservation and environmental issues, Minister Rick Warren convinced many churches across America to screen the film and spread the news to its followers. The movie spread from hand to hand, from profile to profile, and ultimately won that year's Academy Award for Best Documentary Film.

Continuing to ride the momentum of his rising influence, Gore successfully organized Live Earth, a seven-continent, 24-hour sequence of concerts aimed at raising global awareness about climate change. In October 2007, Albert Arnold "Al" Gore won the Nobel Peace Prize for his efforts in leading the world to finally and publicly recognize the existence and importance of the global climate crisis issue. Not only had he successfully gone on for a second act—that second act turned out to be a showstopper.

FROM PASSING FAD TO UNAVOIDABLE TRUTH

Over the last few decades, the Internet has come from out of nowhere and crept up on the way that nearly every company in the world does business. It has gone from passing fad to noted influence to unavoidable truth. As little as ten years ago, many companies were still loath to provide universal e-mail and Internet access for all employees. Today, what once seemed like a passing trend has become an inescapable fact. Who would deny that to compete in the modern marketplace, you absolutely have to be online, and you absolutely have to provide employees with access to e-mail and the Internet? Then again, hindsight is always 20/20.

The companies that have truly and overwhelmingly succeeded in the online arena are the ones that recognized and capitalized on trends at a time when few others even acknowledged that they existed. The dot-com bubble came and went, yet the tools and abilities out of which it was spawned have since become fully integrated into our day-to-day businesses and personal lives. At the heart of it, the message is simple: You need technology to compete.

Social networks are often categorized in the same way that early Internet endeavors were: as a flash in the pan, a temporary fad, an impermanent whim destined to fall by the wayside. Yet businesses fell into this same trap just a decade ago.

The difficulty in capitalizing on social networking lies in viewing it as a fad rather than as the new way that business will be carried out in the future. Nowadays nobody touts the glory of the e-mail system, just as nobody in this day and age is a rabid supporter of the telephone. When the system itself becomes ubiquitous, the technology behind it stops mattering in the slightest. When picking up the phone to call a business partner halfway around the world, nobody ever stops to think, "Wow, this telephone thing is really amazing." The technology has faded into the background, and the importance of that technology has become entirely tied up in the communication that it facilitates. In other words, the way a phone works has become completely inconsequential—as long as I can call my vendor in Beijing, the sequence of satellite transmissions that actually enables that call couldn't matter less.

Likewise, when logging on to a social network for the first time, you can't help but concentrate on how great the new tool is. Still, after weeks and months of steady usage, the tool itself fades into the background and eventually stops mattering at all. Logging on to Facebook or LinkedIn to check on the status of your network ceases to be a new ability provided by a fantastic new technology and simply becomes an essential tool for keeping up with friends and colleagues. You eventually stop thinking about the fact that you're using a social network entirely; all you know is that you're checking in on what everybody is up to today.

CHECKMATE

**IN THE NEW AND EVOLVING ONLINE WORLD,
THE GREATEST MOMENTUM GOES NOT TO THE
CANDIDATE WITH THE MOST DETAILED PLAN FOR
CONQUERING THE WEB BUT TO THE CANDIDATE
WHO SURRENDERS HIS (HER) IMAGE TO THE
CLICKING MASSES, THE SAME WAY A ROCK
GUITARIST MIGHT FALL BACKWARD OFF THE STAGE
INTO THE HANDS OF AN ADORING CROWD.
—MATT BAI, (NEW YORK TIMES MAGAZINE,
DECEMBER 9, 2007, "THE WEB USERS CAMPAIGN.")**

Whether you personally implement a social networking strategy
or hire someone to empower your community through social
networking initiatives, you'll increase your company's internal
and external ROI and get the jump on your competition.
Social tools extend basic social skills and enable proactive
businesspeople to build communities that better connect
employees and customers among themselves and with one
other. By putting yourself and your company at the center of
your immediate universe, you give yourself access to newer
and better information and facilitate better and more effective
communication between you and everybody around you. In so
doing, the legacy thinking taught in business schools is squared
with new ideas and new measures of success. By building
social, cultural, and financial capital through the amplification
of your microcelebrity brand and through successful use of
feedback loops, you might even be able to take it one step
further. Consider the ultimate opportunity made possible
through social networking for business: Take the lead, set the

corporate standard for success, and reinvent legacy thinking for your industry.

Social networking offers you the opportunity to become an expert in your field and lets people near and far know about you and what you do. It makes your connections more visible and more readily available, and can increase your reach and create brand awareness. Does that mean that the more you affect culture, the more you attract financial capital? The answer is yes… to a certain extent. However, just as you can't directly correlate the number of people who will buy your product to the amount of money you spend on marketing and branding it offline, you can't directly correlate sales to your online presence. Whatever your strategy, always keep one rule in mind: Success begins with adding value to your community.

With social networking strategies, just as with general Internet and online strategies before them, it's not as much a slot machine as it is a game of chess. Making a single move probably won't make a fortune pour right into your lap. Ultimately though, planning your moves carefully and being able to think a few moves ahead will pay off in a way that is far greater, far more meaningful, and most importantly, far more lasting than any one-time fluke could ever be. A slot machine is all about luck; a chess game is all about making the best use of strategy given the available possibilities and opportunities. Now it's up to you to get out there and make your first move.

…May the best players win.

33millionpeople.com A blog where the ideas within this book are discussed and where new opportunities are vetted. An online space where the *33 Million People in the Room* community (that's you, along with book contributors and other top business leaders) share successful social networking for business strategies, tactics, and stories.

Bebo A social network founded in 2005 with 40 million registered users. Mainly home to teens and young adults in Canada, England, Ireland, New Zealand, Australia, and Poland. *See page 24.*

BioMedExperts A social network specifically geared toward the scientific community. Allows users to collaborate on medical research and development.

Blog (n.) Short for **Web log**. A Web site normally maintained by an individual (or group of individuals) and updated with regular entries. Entries are typically displayed in chronological order and tagged with relevant keywords and phrases. (v.) To maintain a blog.

Brand Equity The amount of familiarity associated with a brand within its target audience.

GLOSSARY

Center of the Universe Study A 2006 joint research study carried out by UCLA and Boardex concerned with how being in the center of a network affects the financial success of a company.

Club Penguin A social network aimed at children featuring avatars and mini-games.

Cocreation The act or practice of bringing together a group of individuals to collaborate where each person brings his or her unique talents to the project. Can refer to online or offline groups.

Connection Refers to an individual on a shared social network with whom you've both confirmed a shared relationship.

Crowdsourcing The act or practice of taking a task normally completed by a single professional and opening it up to contributions by a group of nonprofessionals.

Cultural Capital The amount of influence an individual carries outside his immediate social circle, in a given industry or in society at large.

Facebook A social network founded in 2004 that connects people with friends, coworkers, and acquaintances. Currently assessed at 124 million members and growing rapidly. *See page 21.*

FAQ Short for Frequently Asked Questions. A section on a Web site where answers to common questions are listed for reference purposes.

Feed A shortened version of a Web document that shows only the most recent updates. Used on social networks to display the most recent updates made to your profile or to the profiles of others in your personal network.

Feedback Loop Refers to the cycle of feedback inherent in online communication. An event on the part of a company or individual leads to feedback on the part of the audience, which in turn leads back to the feedback of the company/individual.

Flickr A social network where users can upload and share photos and images.

Friend *See Connection.*

hi5 A social network founded in 2003 with 70 million registered users. Rated the number-one social network across 25 nations in Latin America, Europe, Asia, and Africa. *See page 22.*

juliettepowell.com A Web site that is home to the blog 33millionpeople, as well as other media, new media, and social media-related activities of the author such as video, TV, radio, and mobile applications.

LinkedIn A social network aimed at business professionals and entrepreneurs. Founded in 2003 and home to 25 million registered users. *See page 25.*

Meet-Up An online social networking portal that facilitates offline group meetings in various localities around the world. Meet-up allows members to find and join groups unified by a common interest.

Microblogging The practice of sending brief (<140 character-long) updates to a blog or microblogging service such as Twitter. Posts are immediate and highly portable via mobile devices and cell phones.

Microcelebrity An individual who has reached a certain amount of fame in a given industry or social group, typically through online resources.

Mini Feed *See Feed.*

Mobile Application In social networking, refers to an application that provides limited access to a given social network's functionality via a cell phone or mobile device.

MySpace A social network founded in 2003 designed to connect individuals with their friends. Currently assessed at 114 million users and growing rapidly. *See page 20.*

News Feed *See Feed.*

Orkut A social network founded by Google in 2004 with 120 million users. Mainly houses users from Brazil and India. *See page 23.*

Post (n.) An updated entry to a Web site, blog, or social network. (v.) The act of updating a Web site, blog, or social network.

Reed's Law A law stating that the effectiveness of large networks (and social networks in particular) can scale exponentially with the size and social importance of the network.

SEO Stands for Search Engine Optimization. Refers to the process of improving a Web site's ranking in search engine results, thereby increasing the number of visitors to the site.

SMS Stands for Short Messaging Service. Refers to text-based messages exchanged between mobile devices and cell phones.

Social Capital A term referring to the extent of your personal network of friends and colleagues and the potential value carried therein.

Social Currency Valued information or collectibles that are shared to reinforce a sense of belonging to a group and that have the benefit of encouraging further social interactions.

Social Influencer A person who is prone to influencing the actions of other individuals in her personal social network via her own actions and ideas.

Social Media Internet-based tools for sharing and discussing information among human beings. The term most often refers to activities that integrate technology, social interaction, and the construction of words, pictures, videos, and audio.

Social Network Classically refers to a community in which individuals are somehow connected (through friendship, values, working relationships, ideas, and so on). The modern definition of the term *social network* also refers to a Web application where people can connect with one another.

Social Networking Platform *See Social Network.*

Status Update A one- to two-sentence description of your activities or thoughts, as posted on a social networking platform.

Strong Tie A relationship between two individuals based on shared experiences or situations, as in close friends or coworkers. *See also Weak Tie.*

Tag (n.) A keyword or term assigned to a Web site, post, or other piece of information that describes the content it contains; allows the tagged information to be easily relocated. (v.) To assign a tag.

TED Stands for the Technology, Entertainment, and Design Conference. An annual invitation-only gathering bringing together some of the world's leading entrepreneurs and creative minds in collaborative presentations that encourage inspiration and innovation.

Traffic The amount of data transferred through the Internet. Used more specifically to refer to the number of users of a given Web site.

Transparency The online practice of keeping data easily accessible and viewable by a Web site's or blog's visitors. Also refers to the difficulty of hiding information that is posted online.

Tweet An update sent out via Twitter.

Twitter A social network and microblogging service popular among heavy users of technology in which frequent updates are posted using mobile devices. *See page 25.*

Virality The widespread dissemination of a message online that mimics a pathological virus in the way it gets passed from one node to the next.

Vlog Short for video blog. A form of blog in which updates and comments are made through posted or linked videos and text.

Wall A feature of a social networking profile that displays a user's recent comments and activities.

Weak Tie A tangential relationship between two individuals based on a one-time meeting or an introduction through friends or coworkers. *See also Strong Tie.*

Webkinz A social network aimed at children featuring virtual versions of plush toys.

Widget A small piece of software that fans can easily embed in their profiles across social networking sites or on Web sites or blogs.

Wiki A collaborative online tool where anybody with access can share and modify information.

Wikipedia An online collaborative peer-produced encyclopedia based on the wiki concept.

YouTube A social network featuring shared video content.

I especially want to thank Jimmy Wales, Andrea Weckerle, Sunny Bates, June Cohen, Chris Anderson, Ori Brafman, Pilar Queen, Dina Kaplan, Amy Shuster, Caroline McCarthy, Gary Vaynerchuk, Tara Hunt, Sarah Lacy, Jeff Pulver, John Perry Barlow, Clay Shirky, Howard Rheingold, Rachel Masters, Toby Daniels, Hilary Rowland, Trina Albus, Daniel Laporte, David Bankston, Jed Alpert, Kenny Miller, Anita Ondine Smith, Ian McFarland, Astro Teller, Naomi Kent, Mike Spencer, Aviva Mohilner, Kitt Gant, and Amos and Shaun Pilot for affording me the privilege of your experience and guidance.

My heartfelt thanks to Chris Brogan and Lawrence Leson for encouraging me to write this book and my deepest appreciation to my community of friends, including Abby Schneiderman, Ilana Arazie, Oz Sultan, Brett Petersel, Caroline Wexler, Mike Hudack, Andrew A. Rosen, Warren L. Habib, Jack Hidary, Bill Sobel, University at Albany's Professor Fogelman and his School of Business fall '08 students, Nicolas Cienca, Matt Sitomer, Jon Benjamin, Unjoo Na, Greg Sonbuchner, Adam Dell, Gary Rabkin, Aviva Mohilner, David Thorpe, Matthew Greenhouse, Charles McCoy, Joel Dreyfuss, and Alain Simard, as well as to my Cirque du Soleil, MuchMusic, and MusiquePlus friends. And who could forget Jonathan Askin (he asked for a mention so he can show this book to potential girlfriends and get some street cred), Chandra Prakash (the teacher who never gave up on me), and Chris Demers (who appeared in my life just in time to

ACKNOWLEDGMENTS

remind me why I started writing in the first place)? Thank you all! It is a privilege to be sharing the same sky with all of you.

To Amy Neidlinger and Tim Moore at FT Press, special thanks for believing in me and for helping to get this first-time author published through it all.

Finally, 33 million thank you's to my Facebook friends and to my fellow Gatherists for your suggestions and advice. And to you, the reader, we'd love to get your feedback and hear your stories, so come join the conversation at 33millionpeople.com.

Warm Regards,
Juliette

A

B

INDEX

F

G

GBN (Global Business Network), xii

Geek Squad, 112-115

Gehry, Frank, 3

genuineness. *See* authenticity

Gibson, William, 104

Gladwell, Malcolm, 95

Global Business Network (GBN), xii

global warming, Al Gore and, 122-126

Goldcorp, 105-106

Gore, Albert Arnold "Al," 122-126

Groening, Matt, 3

H-I

Harvard University, 21

Hawk, Thomas, 65-66

hi5, 22-23

Horowitz, Bradley, 31

HorsePigCow, 83

Howe, Jeff, 106

Hunt, Tara, 16-19, 83

importance of social networks, 6-8, 127-128

An Inconvenient Truth, 122-126

Indian social networks, Orkut, 23-24

influence, achieving through social networks

　　case studies

　　　　Jimmy Wales, 46-48

　　　　Johnny Chung Lee, 42-44

O

Obama, Barack, 86-92

Once You're Lucky, Twice You're Good: The Rebirth of Silicon Valley and the Rise of Web 2.0 (Lacy), 63

one-off, crowdsourcing as, 105-106

online persona, managing, 32-40

    Facebook, 35-39

    LinkedIn, 34-35

    mobile applications, 39-40

    overview, 33-34

Orkut, 23-24

P

PayPal, 3

persona. *See* online persona

Polish social networks, Bebo, 24

posting items on Facebook, 37

power of social networks, 129-130

PriceRitePhoto, 65-67

privacy, 40-41

production opportunities

    crowdsourcing

        advantages of, 104-105

        case study: Threadless, 100-103

        compared to cocreation, 108

        crowdsourcing a dedicated community, 106-107

        as one-off, 105-106

    customer cocreation, 107-109

FT Press

FINANCIAL TIMES

In an increasingly competitive world, it is quality
of thinking that gives an edge—an idea that opens new
doors, a technique that solves a problem, or an insight
that simply helps make sense of it all.

We work with leading authors in the various arenas
of business and finance to bring cutting-edge thinking
and best-learning practices to a global market.

It is our goal to create world-class print publications
and electronic products that give readers
knowledge and understanding that can then be
applied, whether studying or at work.

To find out more about our business
products, you can visit us at www.ftpress.com.